The Vinegar Home Guide

by Emily Thacker

Published by:

Tresco Publishers

718 - 12th Street N.W.

Canton, Ohio 44703

U.S.A.

What Kind Of Vinegar Do I Use?

Most cleaning chores call for white vinegar. Some food recipes call for white vinegar, others are better with apple cider (or even herbal or wine) vinegar. In most cases, the difference in vinegars is one of taste and aroma, not of effectiveness. In this volume, if a specific type of vinegar is best in a particular circumstance, the cleaning tip or recipe specifies the kind. If the kind of vinegar is not indicated, either white or apple cider vinegar may be used — the choice is yours!

ISBN: 1-883944-09-0

Printing 12 11 10 9 8 7 6 5 4 3 2

Fourth Edition   Copyright 1996   Tresco Publishers

Table of Contents

INTRODUCTION i

CHAPTER ONE
What Is Vinegar? 5

CHAPTER TWO
General Cleaning 11

CHAPTER THREE
In The Kitchen 18

CHAPTER FOUR
In The Bathroom, Bedroom & Office 27

CHAPTER FIVE
Vinegar Goes Outside 32

CHAPTER SIX
Vinegar Is For People 36

CHAPTER SEVEN
Vinegar & Laundry 42

CHAPTER EIGHT
Cooking With Vinegar 51

CHAPTER NINE
Odds & Ends 56

Dear Reader,

When the original volume of "Home Remedies from the Old South" came out, many kind readers wrote to me expressing interest and enclosing questions on the usefulness of apple cider vinegar. These letters led to "The Vinegar Book."

Now, my mail shows my readers have many unanswered questions about how vinegar cleans, and about how it can be used around the home. So, in an attempt to answer these requests for information, "The Vinegar Home Guide" has come into being.

Over the years, my fascination with all the things vinegar can do encouraged me to gather a collection of cleaning and cooking lore. Many of these hints and tips work wonders — in a particular cleaning situation. In other circumstances they may be ineffective. A lot depends on the cleaning chore. I invite you to enjoy reading the cleaning remedies in this book to see how others have used vinegar. Then, I encourage you to experiment to find what works for you.

Some of my earliest memories are of my Grandfather gathering up apples to take to my Uncle John's apple press. The exact mix of apples was more art than science, and a closely held secret. There were always a few sweet, aromatic apples, some spicy ones to add flavor, and a nice bunch of tart ones to give the mixture body.

The apples were washed and ground up, then pressed in a mill powered by horses walking in a circle. The fresh sweet cider was delicious, but that was just the beginning. When it 'turned' and became hard, it was time to make apple cider vinegar in big old wooden barrels. The vinegar was used for preserving, cleaning and disinfecting. Since then, I've learned that, even today, hospitals use vinegar for killing germs and to fight children's ear infections.

I believe it was the German poet Goethe who wrote, "If everyone would sweep the street in front of their own house, the whole world would be clean." To rephrase that philosophy, I believe that if we each protect our little corner of the earth, the whole planet will be safe. To this end, most of the cleaning tips in this volume recommend using scraps of old cloth for cleaning rather than paper towels. Paper cleaning products are handy things, and wonderful for really nasty cleanups. But please remember, every time you use a paper towel, somewhere, a tree is cut down. Besides, cloth is reusable and so is less expensive, as well as being softer and less likely to scratch fine finishes!

Please remember, this book is an attempt to share information. Many old-time ways are not best for today. And yet, many of the old ways are well worth the trouble to try them. They do not disturb the environment, set off allergic reactions, pollute the air we breathe or deliver harsh chemicals to skin and air. Wishing you all the best,

Emily

Chapter One

What Is Vinegar?

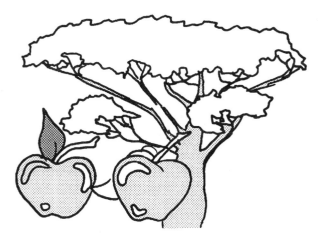

Soon after the first person played a flute in ancient Egypt—

About the time sheep were first domesticated in the Near East—

And Europeans were learning to eat honey and catch fish in nets of hair—

Before the first dogs were domesticated in the British Isles—

—Mankind discovered that a very useful, sour liquid formed when a mildly alcoholic beverage was allowed to set out, exposed to air. Vinegar came into being! And for more than 10,000 years it has been one of the most useful and widely distributed liquids on the planet.

The English word "vinegar" comes from the French word "vinaigre," which accurately describes the origin of this delightful liquid. "Vin" is for the wine the first vinegar was made from — and "aigre" to acknowledge the fact that the wine had turned sour. Vin - gar is, literally, soured wine.

When a sweet liquid, such as apple or grape juice, is sealed up and allowed to ferment (away from air) the sugar in it is changed into alcohol. If this liquid is permitted to ferment for a second time (this time in the presence of air) the alcohol is transformed into acetic acid.

While the very first vinegar came from the natural souring of fermented wine, it soon became such a prized product that mankind learned how to make it intentionally. Since then it has been used as a flavor enhancing condiment, a preservative, and as a cleaning agent for people, pets and objects around the home.

To make vinegar, all that is required is a juice (or sweetened water) with enough sugar content to produce at least a 6% to 10% alcoholic liquid in the first fermentation action. Old-time "slow process" vinegar needs

5

about a 10% alcohol content to get the second fermentation process going. Newer, "fast process" vinegar can be made from a liquid with only about 6% alcohol.

Vinegar is made from many substances. For industrial uses, acetic acid which has been manufactured from wood products is diluted to make a kind of vinegar. At one time this colorless product was colored with caramel and sold as table grade vinegar, although its food value and aroma were inferior to fruit based vinegar. Today, this adulterated vinegar is rarely sold as a food.

Vinegar for table use is made in nearly every country, all across the world. The food product which is used to make vinegar depends, mostly, on where it is made.

In the United States, much of the vinegar intended for table use is made from apples, producing apple cider vinegar. England is famous for its malt vinegar, made from grain. France is noted for its wine vinegar, made from grapes, while Japan and China specialize in vinegar made from rice. Vinegar is made from many natural products, including:

- Apples
- Bananas
- Barley
- Blackberries
- Grapes
- Honey
- Molasses
- Potatoes
- Raspberries
- Rice
- Strawberries
- Wood Shavings

After vinegar is made it is often combined with herbs and spices, or even specially aged in wood kegs. Any kind of vinegar — white, apple cider, wine, malt, etc. — may be enhanced this way.

KINDS OF VINEGAR

Distilled, or "white" vinegar is usually used for cleaning. Because white vinegar is a colorless liquid it is less likely to discolor articles being cleaned. Generally, white vinegar is made from wood or grain, and has a consistent 5% acetic acid content.

White vinegar is often used for pickling, salad dressings, marinating, and for preparing foods when the distinctive flavor of other vinegars is not wanted. It is a reliable, consistent, inexpensive and widely available product.

For most cooking, when special flavor is wanted, or for personal use, other kinds of vinegar are usually used. Apple cider is widely available, inexpensive, has a long history of health uses and has a fresh, distinctive flavor.

Herbal and balsamic vinegars are more expensive and harder to find. Balsamic vinegar is aged in wood, often for several years. It is considered one of the finest flavorings available for many foods. Herbal vinegars can usually be found in health food stores, Or, they can be prepared from white, apple cider, or wine vinegar.*

Vinegars made by old, slower processes are known for their fine aromas and have more subtle flavors than ones made by newer, faster processes. Aromatic vinegars have spices and herbs added to them. They produce a fragrant liquid which is used in the kitchen and in personal care products such as after shave lotions and skin fresheners.

Some of the first 'toilet waters' were aromatic vinegars.

HOW VINEGAR CLEANS

In many parts of the country, water for the home comes from underground sources. When this water runs through underground reservoirs it can dissolve minerals out of rock formations. Limestone, which is mostly calcium carbonate, dissolves especially easily.

This "hard" water carries the dissolved limestone until it finds an object to deposit it on. The inside of plumbing pipes, bathroom and kitchen fixtures, shower walls and curtains, and washer lint traps encourage minerals to precipitate out of water. These minerals show up as a rock-hard coating which can be difficult to clean without scratching metal surfaces.

In a short time these hard water minerals build up into a dirty white scale on bathroom and kitchen surfaces. This is the same stuff that produces stalagmites and stalactites in limestone caves. And it can be just as hard as these natural wonders, but it is not nearly as pretty!

See chapter on cooking with vinegar.

Fortunately, vinegar dissolves calcium carbonate, as well as scale from other minerals. Tradition says Hannibal, a general from Carthage (in North Africa), used the fact that vinegar weakens rock in his march over the Alps from Spain to Italy.

Supposedly, Hannibal's soldiers poured vinegar over heated boulders. This weakened the stones enough that they could be broken up and removed from mountain trails, allowing Hannibal to move his elephants over the narrow mountain trails.

Today, the fact that vinegar wears down and destroys rock formations is important, because this makes it a nearly perfect cleaner for removing mineral accumulations from bathroom and kitchen fixtures. Even though vinegar is good at dissolving minerals, it is non-poisonous and gentle on hands.

VINEGAR ACTS AGAINST GERMS

Vinegar contains a host of germ fighting components. It is has both antibiotic and antiseptic properties. And, it can contain natural tannins which help to preserve foods. Vinegar not only can kill bacteria, its presence slows its ability to grow back.

One of the best things about cleaning with vinegar is its action on mold and mildew. Mold and mildew are not dirt. They are living, plantlike growths. That means cleaning the part that shows is not enough to get rid of them. These fungus growths have to be killed, all the way to their roots, or they will immediately grow back.

And that is why vinegar is such a good cleaning product. It has the ability to actually kill mold and mildew spores that cause new growth.

Vinegar is a completely biodegradable product. Nature can easily break it down into components that feed and nurture plant life. This makes it superior to chemical cleaners that poison the soil today, and remain in it and destroy plant life for many years.

HOW TO CHOOSE A VINEGAR

Most cleaning and laundry chores call for white vinegar. It has a mild odor and does not have anything in it to leave a stain on fabrics. Apple cider vinegar is a good choice for cleaning that calls for giving the air a

Mushrooms & truffles are in the mold & mildew family!

pleasant, apple-fresh scent. Either one leaves a room smelling as if it has just been cleaned.

Throughout this book, whenever a cleaning tip does not specify the kind of vinegar to be used, white vinegar is usually the best one to use. But, it is always possible to do the cleaning chore with any kind of vinegar. The choice is always yours!

WHEN TO CLEAN WITH VINEGAR

Vinegar is the cleaner of choice for those with allergies, asthma or a sensitivity to harsh chemicals. It also appeals to those who are interested in protecting the environment from pollution, and is the cleaning product of choice for the thrifty consumer.

Vinegar's acid character makes it especially useful for neutralizing the effect of alkaline-based cleaning products. This includes most soaps and detergents. Vinegar also has the ability to dissolve the dulling film these products can leave behind.

Copper (and compounds which contain copper) can be cleaned with vinegar. When metal develops a green tarnish it usually means there is copper in it. This green coating can be seen on objects that are 100% copper, as well as on copper compounds such as brass and bronze.

Brass can develop a dull, greenish discoloration because it is mostly copper, with some zinc mixed into it. Bronze also has a copper base. The copper in bronze is mixed with tin (and sometimes a bit of zinc, too).

WHEN NOT TO CLEAN WITH VINEGAR

Just as important as when to use vinegar, is when not to use it. Because, like all good things, vinegar should not be used on some things.

Vinegar will tarnish silver, so never expose it to vinegar, unless you want it to instantly look old and dirty. And, never soak pearls in vinegar, as it will dissolve them!

If you reuse plastic bags, such as bread wrappers, never turn the bag inside-out, so that a food with vinegar in it touches the colored ink of the bag label design. Many have dyes that release lead into food when soaked in vinegar.

HOW TO CLEAN WITH VINEGAR

Vinegar is a cost efficient cleaner, so be generous with it. In general, begin cleaning by removing loose dirt with a sweeper, brush, dust cloth, or just shake it off. Then scrape or peel off any lumps or globs of dirt. Remove what remains with detergent, water and white vinegar.

For best results, keep your cleaning equipment clean. The best cleaning machine in the house is usually that old toothbrush that reaches all the places nothing else will. Rinse it out once in a while in full strength vinegar, shake it partly dry, and then allow it to dry in the sun.

CAUTIONS

ALWAYS test a small, inconspicuous area of fabrics, wall coverings, flooring, etc. before using any cleaning product — including vinegar.

No product, even one as safe and gentle as vinegar, is safe for every person or every situation. While vinegar has been safely used for thousands of years, it is possible for certain individuals to be sensitive to it. If there is any possibility that you may be sensitive or allergic to vinegar, consult a medical professional before exposing your skin to it.

When cleaning copper, always dispose of all cleaning cloths or paper towels as soon as the job is finished — that green tarnish on copper is poisonous!

Chapter Two

General Cleaning

Vinegar is an acid based cleaner. This makes it especially good for taking out stains made by coffee and tea, lifting rust and lime deposits, cleaning stains made by condiments such as mustard or catsup, and removing wine or stains made by alcohol based liquids. Used this way, white vinegar acts as a very mild bleach.

And, because vinegar is acid, it is a good final, neutralizing rinse after using alkaline cleaning solutions such as detergents and soaps (including dishwasher soaps), wax strippers, drain and oven cleaners. A final vinegar rinse in the washing machine helps colored clothing stay bright, because vinegar helps remove lingering traces of detergents and the film left by soaps.

In addition, vinegar helps water sheet off glassware, so it helps prevent water spots on dishes and streaks on windows. Some more specific ways people have suggested using vinegar in general cleaning follow:

Vinegar Wet Wipes
Mix 3 tablespoons white vinegar and 1 teaspoon liquid detergent in a bowl with 2 cups of water. Wet small pieces of clean, soft cloth (6 to 10 inch squares) in the vinegar mixture, then wring them out. Place the cloths in a tightly capped container. Whenever there is a need for a quick cleanup, use one of these wet wipes.

Vinegar wet wipes are good for touch-ups on windows, spots on mirrors, and cleaning faucets, door knobs, sinks, counter tops, appliances and light switches.

Dirty Ashtrays
Spray full strength vinegar on ashtrays with heavy stains or encrusted dirt and allow them to set for 5 minutes. Wipe the dirt out and spray again to remove lingering odors.

Sweeter Smelling Ashtrays

Reduce ashtray odor by spraying clean, polished ashtrays with apple cider vinegar. Begin by wiping the inside of a clean ashtray with a wax-based furniture polish. (This will help to keep odors from penetrating.) When the wax is dry, spray the ashtray with apple cider vinegar and allow it to dry without wiping.

Mild Brass Cleaner

1/4	cup vinegar	2	cups water
1/4	cup liquid detergent		
1/8	cup salt		

Put all the ingredients together and stir until the salt is dissolved. Wipe the liquid on tarnished brass, then immediately wipe it off. Polish with a soft cloth until completely dry. Apply a coating of creamy car wax and buff to keep brass clean longer.

Water-Stained Carpet

When jute-backed carpet gets wet, the brown coloring in the backing is released. It runs into the fibers in the front of the carpet, where it shows up as a brown or yellow stain. Neutralize jute stains by dampening the stains with a mixture of 1/4 cup white vinegar and 1 cup water. Immediately blot the carpet dry. One or two applications should remove the stain.

Gentle All-Purpose Cleaner

Fill a spray bottle almost full of water, then add 1/4 cup white vinegar and 3 tablespoons liquid detergent (the kind used to wash dishes by hand). Use a few squirts of this gentle liquid to clean away light dust and dirt before moisture in the air turns them into a sticky film that is more difficult to remove. Use this gentle all-purpose cleaner on chair railings, window frames, baseboards, anywhere dust or dirt accumulate.

Doorknobs

Some of the dirtiest places in the home (and most forgotten hiding places for germs) are the doorknobs. Most will benefit from an occasional cleaning with a cloth dampened in vinegar. It will kill germs and wipe away dirt. Glass doorknobs will sparkle like new!

Glass or Plastic Beads

Dip strands of beads in a quart of warm water to which 1 teaspoon liquid detergent has been mixed. Rinse in another quart of water to which 1 tablespoon white vinegar has been added. Blot dry with a towel, then finish drying with a hair dryer, set to low heat.

Sanitize The Telephone

Germs that cause colds and flu live on surfaces which are handled by many members of the household. Wipe the telephone receiver down with full strength vinegar to kill any bacteria which may be breeding on it.

Air Freshener

Pure white vinegar makes a great freshener for stale air. Simply use a pump spray to deliver a fine mist to musty areas or to remove cooking or smoking odors. For a fresher scent, use apple cider vinegar.

Scented Air Freshener

Fill a pump spray bottle with well-strained herbal vinegar and use to both cleanse the air and to add refreshing, natural scents. Often these scented air fresheners do not cause the allergic sniffles and sneezes some people experience when using commercial fresheners.

Broom Revitalizer

Old plastic brooms (and cornstalk ones, too) can be reshaped and deodorized by soaking them in a bucket of very hot water, to which a cup of apple cider vinegar has been added. Let the bristles soak for at least 10 minutes, then shake the broom to remove most of the water. Wrap two or three large rubber bands around the bristles and set the broom in the sun for several hours. When the rubber bands are removed the broom will retain its new, neat shape. And best of all, it will smell fresh and clean!

'New' Stubby Broom

When a broom is finally ready to be discarded, try cutting about half the length of the bristles off. Angle the cut so that the bristles on the short side are about 1 inch in length and the ones on the long side about are about 5 inches in length. Soak the broom as above, shake it out and set in the sun until dry. This 'new' stubby broom will do a great job in corners and other places that are hard to reach with a regular broom. And, the long handle will save the bending and crawling that using a regular whisk broom requires.

One-Pass Sweeping

A broom will pick up more dust if it is sprayed with vinegar water. Just put a cup of warm water in a pump spray bottle and add 1 cup vinegar. Spray the broom before using, and occasionally during use.

Louvered Doors and Shutters

Remove dirt, dust and musty odors from louvered surfaces with vinegar and a paint stirring stick (available, free, at most paint stores). Simply wrap a soft cloth over the end of the flat stick, spray it with vinegar, then run it over and under each louver.

Revitalize and Deodorize Drapes

Remove musty or smoky odors from drapes — and take out fine wrinkles at the same time! Mix 1 tablespoon white vinegar with 2 cups warm water and place the mixture in a pump spray bottle. Set to 'fine mist' and spritz each drapery panel lightly, without removing the drapes from the windows. As they dry, most wrinkles will disappear, along with stale odors.

Fiberglass Drapes

Fiberglass is, in many ways, a wonderful material. But when it comes time to wash drapes, fiberglass requires great care. These drapes must never be washed in the washing machine, or put in the dryer! The agitation of the washer, and the tumbling of the dryer, will break, crack and pulverize the glass fibers.

Not only will washing machines and dryers weaken (and eventually destroy) the drapes, tiny fiberglass particles will be deposited in the appliances. These little pieces of glass will cause great itching and irritation for anyone who wears clothes exposed to them.

Wash fiberglass drapes by hanging them on a clothes line and spraying them, gently, with a hose. Follow with a spray of vinegar and water from a pump spray bottle (1 tablespoon of vinegar to each 2 cups of water). This will keep them smelling fresh and clean.

If it is inconvenient to hang fiberglass drapes outside, they may be dipped in a laundry tub of sudsy water, rinsed in clear water, then dipped in a mild vinegar and water solution. Remember to THOROUGHLY rinse out the laundry tub after washing fiberglass drapes!

Fireplace Ashes

A vinegar spray can keep fireplace ashes from flying all over the house when they are cleaned out. Simply spray the ashes with vinegar and water before beginning (1 tablespoon vinegar to 2 cups water). Shovel ashes onto newspapers which have also been dampened with water and vinegar. Continue to spray the ashes every so often and flying dust particles will be prevented.

Putting vinegar on the ashes also helps to neutralize this strong alkali. Prevent alkali burns on hands by rinsing in water and vinegar as soon as the job is finished. Rinse any tools used, too.

Brighten Lights

Get the most from your lighting dollars by keeping light bulbs clean and free of dust and dirt. Wipe cool bulbs with a cloth dampened in vinegar water (1 tablespoon vinegar to a quart of water). Always clean bulbs with current turned OFF!

Grandmother got lye by soaking wood ashes in water.

Light fixtures, chimneys, reflectors, and diffusers also need to be cleaned regularly. Dip them in sudsy water, then rinse in water with some white vinegar added to it. As with light bulbs, always clean AFTER they have completely cooled!

Use a mild vinegar and water solution for plastic parts, a strong one for glass items.

Mop Magic
For stay-shiny-longer floors, make this special glossy surface cleaning solution. To a bucket of warm water, add 1/2 cup fabric softener and 1/4 cup vinegar. Mop as usual and watch the magic shine appear. This works best for lightly soiled floors.

Waxing Floors
Make your floor wax go on smoother, last longer, and shine better by rinsing the floor with a strong solution of water and white vinegar before applying the wax. A cup of vinegar to a half bucket of warm water is about right.

Quick Pick-Up For No-Wax Floors
Mix white vinegar and water, half and half, in a pump spray bottle. Mist the traffic areas of no-wax flooring and immediately buff dry with an old towel. This quick pickup will have the floor looking shiny clean in about two minutes!

Cleaning Waxed Floors
Ammonia and heat both remove wax. Preserve wax surfaces when cleaning by using cool water and a vinegar rinse. This will make the shine last longer.

Really Dirty Vinyl Floors
Pre-treating really dirty vinyl floors can make the job of cleaning them easier. Spray full strength vinegar on spots, globs and sticky areas. Let set for 5 minutes, then mop as usual.

Ballpoint Ink
Pen marks on painted walls and woodwork can often be lifted by soaking them in white vinegar. Dribble full strength vinegar on marks and allow to soak for 10 to 15 minutes. Marks on vertical surfaces can be soaked by draping a vinegar-damped cloth over them.

Walls

Wash painted walls with a gentle detergent and then rinse in warm water and white vinegar. Add 1/2 cup vinegar to half a bucket of water.

Ceilings

Lightly soiled ceilings can be washed and rinsed in one operation. To half a bucket of water, add 1 tablespoon liquid dish detergent and 1/2 cup white vinegar. Wipe a 3 foot square of ceiling clean, then dry with a soft cloth to prevent streaking.

Glass and Ceramic Candlesticks

Soak glass and ceramic candlesticks in very warm water with plenty of detergent in it. Wipe wax residue off with a soft cloth or sponge. Then, rinse in hot water with a bit of white vinegar in it. Put a coating of oil in the candle-holding well to make it easier to remove old candles.

Lamp Shades

Before throwing a hopelessly stained or misshapen lamp shade away, you might want to give it a chance to redeem itself. Make a sudsy solution of white vinegar, liquid detergent, and lukewarm water in a laundry tub. Immerse the end of the shade with the heaviest soil buildup first. Swish it around a little, then turn the lamp shade over, with the opposite end submerged in the water. Turn the shade over and repeat the process. Swish it around again and drain the water out of the laundry tub. Fill the tub with cool water, add 1 cup white vinegar, and rinse the shade thoroughly. Blot most of the water from the lamp shade and finish drying out of the sun, and without heat.

Old Windows

When window glass seems dull and 'old' looking, it is usually because soap scum and hard water minerals have been allowed to build up on it. Vinegar is very good at cutting through the haze and restoring the shine to such window glass. Use a strong vinegar and water solution, or even full strength vinegar, to remove soap scum and hard water minerals.

Streaky Windows

Streaks are often caused by the sun heating the glass, making the cleaning solution dry too fast. Wash windows on a cloudy day to minimize sun streaking. Or, wash windows on the shady side of the house, then wait for the sun to move. Using a squeegee to remove the cleaning solution will also minimize streaking.

Stretched out areas can be shrunk with hair dryer heat.

Mildewy Windows

Windows that are frequently damp can grow mildew and mold in their corners and on their frames. Use full strength white vinegar to remove all traces of mildew and mold. Any spores that are missed will encourage its fast return.

Good Window Cleaner

1	tablespoon white vinegar	2	drops liquid detergent
1	tablespoon ammonia	1	cup water

Mix all ingredients together and store in a pump spray bottle. Spray onto windows and wipe off with wadded up newspaper or a soft cloth.

Sparkling Window Cleaner

1	tablespoon white vinegar	1	teaspoon cornstarch
1	tablespoon ammonia	2	drops liquid detergent

Add 1 cup water and store in a pump spray bottle. Shake before spraying onto windows, then wipe off with wadded up newspaper or a soft cloth.

Film-Free Window Washing

Outside windows that have their frames painted with latex paint, and windows in homes where the siding is painted with latex paint, often pick up a cloudy film. This is because of the natural sloughing-off process of this kind of paint.

Soaps and detergents do not dissolve this fine coating of latex. Rinsing windows in water with lots of white vinegar in it neutralizes the film and helps to keep the glass clear and clean.

Mirrors

Clean mirrors by spraying a white vinegar and water solution onto a cloth and wiping the mirror with the cloth. Never spray ANY liquid onto a mirror. Dampness can get to the silvering on the mirror's back and cause it to flake or peel away.

Glass Spots

Splatters, spots and isolated fingerprints on windows and mirrors can be removed by wiping them down with vinegar wet wipes. (See the first page of this chapter.)

Chapter Three

In The Kitchen

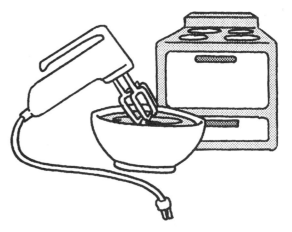

Grandmother knew the value of vinegar in the kitchen, and she used it for more than cooking! All sorts of viruses, bacteria and fungus can grow on kitchen surfaces. Keeping everything clean and dry helps to eliminate them and the sickness they can bring. Vinegar can be big a help in doing this.

Use white vinegar for its antibiotic and antiseptic qualities —

Use apple cider vinegar to add the fresh aroma of ripe fall apples to vinegar's power —

— Or, for a very special effect, clean with your own homemade herbal vinegar!* Herbal vinegar can add a very special aroma to your kitchen, a hint of the best of the foods prepared in your kitchen.

Waxed Surfaces

Clean waxed surfaces with vinegar, instead of ammonia-based products, because ammonia dissolves wax. Also, use cool water to keep the wax hard. Hot water softens wax and makes it easier for tiny particles of dirt to become embedded in it, rather than being washed off.

Miscellaneous Glassware

When soap scum and hard water minerals build up on drinking glasses, vases, mixing bowls, cups, etc., it makes them look old and dull. A good soaking in full strength white vinegar will dissolve the hazy film and bring back their natural, clear beauty.

To clean dull glassware, immerse pieces in a container filled with white vinegar. Let soak for 30 minutes, then scrub with a soft brush dipped in warm, sudsy water. Rinse in clear water, then rinse again in a sink full of very warm water with 1/2 cup white vinegar added to it. Dry with a soft cloth and see how your glassware sparkles!

*See chapter on cooking with vinegar for herbal vinegars.

Lead Crystal

Fine crystal should always be washed and dried by hand. A bit of white vinegar in the rinse water will help keep them from developing a scummy buildup of dulling minerals. To wash: place a rubber mat (or a dish towel) in the bottom of the sink. Add enough hot water and detergent to make enough nice sudsy water to allow you to completely submerge each piece. Wash thoroughly and rinse in hot water with several tablespoons of white vinegar added to it. Dry with a very absorbent cotton towel.

Fine China

When hand washing good dishes, a splash of white vinegar in the last rinse will help prevent streaks and spots - but only use it on china that does not have gold or silver trim. Vinegar can cause metal trims on china to discolor. After drying plates, slip an inexpensive paper plate between each piece of china and you will reduce the chance of dishes being chipped.

Ceramic Dishes, Bowls & Casseroles

Clean encrusted foods from ceramic cookware by scouring them with a nylon scrubber dipped in white vinegar.

Vase Cleaning

Small vases often have tiny openings that make cleaning difficult. Use a small brush dipped in full strength white vinegar to scrub them clean.

Better Vase Cleaning

If you do not have exactly the right size brush for scrubbing the inside of a small vase, use vinegar, water and rice to scour it. Put a handful of rice in the vase and fill it 1/3 of the way full with a half and half mixture of white vinegar and cold water. Shake well, let set for 30 seconds, shake again. Empty out the rice and liquid, rinse in water and vinegar, and set the vase upside down to dry.

Even Better Vase Cleaning

For really tough cleaning jobs, put a few tablespoons of fine sand in a dirty vase. Fill to 1/3 full with a mixture of half white vinegar and half hot water. Shake until deposits are removed, empty and rinse well before drying.

Enamel Ware

Bleach stains from enamel cookware by boiling a few cups of white vinegar in them.

'Silver' trim on china is almost always made of platinum!

Sanitize Cutting Boards

Disinfect wood cutting boards at least once a week (and after each time they are used to cut meat) by applying a liberal coating of salt. Let the salt set for 5 minutes, then wash with 1/2 cup vinegar. This keeps cutting boards sweet-smelling and sanitary. Traditional wood boards should be wiped down with vegetable oil once in a while, too.

Black Appliances

Black (and dark colored) appliances are a special challenge to keep clean, as they reflect every smudge and fingerprint. And, every bit of cleaning solution residue will show up as a streak or hazy film. The secret to keeping these appliances shiny is to clean them often - and to use vinegar as a rinse to remove the film of soapy residue. After washing the appliance, spray full strength white vinegar onto a soft, lint-free cloth. Wipe the appliance surface with the vinegar dampened cloth, then buff with a dry cloth.

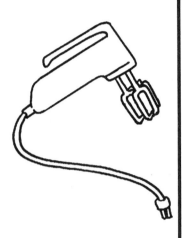

Appliance Cords

Keep electric cords, especially white ones, clean and free of food smears by wiping them frequently with a cloth dampened with white vinegar. (Always unplug electric cords before cleaning them!)

Small Appliances

Can openers, toasters, mixers, blenders and such can be wiped down with a cloth wrung out of white vinegar, then buffed dry. They will stay nice looking longer, and work better, if kept clean.

Always spray vinegar on a cloth (or use a cloth wrung out of vinegar), never spray the appliance directly. Liquid could enter the air vents over motors and damage internal parts. (ALWAYS unplug appliances before cleaning.)

Blender Buttons

White vinegar, on a cotton swab, does a good job of cleaning push buttons and control knobs on blenders and food processors. Rub the vinegar into the small spaces around and between buttons, too.

Mixers

One of the hardest cleaning jobs in the kitchen is getting food splashes off of the underside of mixers. Make this chore easier by wrapping a vinegar dampened cloth around the mixer for a few minutes. Wipe off loose dirt, repeat if necessary.

Can Opener Cleaning

Can opener blades often harbor dried-on food and bits of unidentified gunk, even in the most spotless of kitchens. Soak removable blades in white vinegar until the encrusted food is soft enough to scrub off.

Use a vinegar dampened cotton swab to clean the air vents over the motor, being careful not to push dried food into the motor housing.

Microwave Cleaning Magic

Soften cooked-on food particles by placing a heat safe bowl containing 1/2 cup water and 1/2 cup vinegar in the oven. Heat until the solution begins to boil, then run the microwave, on its highest setting, for 30 seconds. Spills and caked-on foods will wipe off with ease.

Microwave Odor Remover

Place a cup of water to which 2 tablespoons apple cider vinegar have been added in the microwave. Bring the mixture to a boil and then let it set for 3 minutes. The oven will smell fresh and clean again. This is especially good for removing odors from the air after cooking fish or popcorn.

Electric Knives

Wipe all surfaces with a cloth wrung out of a solution of sudsy water and vinegar. Give special attention to crevices around blade mounting areas. Finish by wiping the electric cord and wall plug.

Sharpen Knives

Need to sharpen a knife in a hurry? Spray vinegar onto the bottom of a clay flower pot. Then use the edge of the pot as a whetstone.

Self-Defrosting Refrigerators

The water collecting tray under self-defrosting refrigerators and freezers should be washed occasionally in soapy water. Any buildup of minerals should be dissolved with white vinegar. A teaspoon or two of vinegar in the tray will retard the growth of bacteria and help prevent moldy smells.

Really Dirty Refrigerators

The top of tall appliances such as refrigerators and some freezers can collect a layer of gummy dirt. Dust settles up there, gets mixed with grease in the air and then steam from cooking cements it together into a cleaning challenge.

Vacuum as much of the gunk up as possible. Then spray a damp sponge with full strength vinegar and drizzle liquid for hand washing dishes over the vinegar. Pat the sponge over the entire refrigerator top and let it soak for 15 minutes. Use the sponge to wipe the stuck-on dirt off. (It will come off easily now.) Rinse with a solution of hot water and a dash of white vinegar, then buff dry.

A light coating of wax or polish on the top of the refrigerator will help to keep greasy dust from sticking to it.

Gas Stove Grates

Boil iron burner grates from gas stoves, for about 10 minutes, in water with a cup of vinegar added to it. They will be much easier to clean.

Stove Tops
Wipe spatters and grease from stove tops with a cloth wrung out of a solution made from 1/2 cup white vinegar, 1/2 cup water, and 1 teaspoon liquid detergent.

Oven Cleaner
Put 3 cups of water into a shallow baking dish and heat oven to 300°. Turn the oven off and let set for 20 minutes. Replace the water with 2 cups of ammonia and allow to set overnight. To 1/2 cup of the ammonia, add 1/2 cup white vinegar and 2 cups baking soda. Smooth this mixture over oven surfaces and allow to set for 20 minutes. Wipe away the cleaner and rinse with clear water.

Oven Racks
Spray oven racks with vinegar and let set until they dry naturally. Then place them in a tub of very hot water with 1 cup of vinegar and a tablespoon of dishwasher detergent added to it. Let the racks soak until the water has cooled. Repeat soaking process and then wipe the racks down with a sponge.

Dishwashers
Dishwashers, especially those used in hard water areas, often attract an unsightly buildup of lime and other minerals. In addition to discoloring the inside of the dishwasher, minerals can damage its working parts. These deposits can be dissolved by running the dishwasher for a complete washing cycle, with no detergent in it. Instead, put 2 cups white vinegar in the bottom of the dishwasher. Stop the machine before the drying cycle begins and wipe the top and sides down with a soft cloth.

Never dry the bottom of the dishwasher, as many brands rely on a small amount of water remaining in the bottom to protect seals from drying out and being ruined.

Quick Kitchen Deodorizing Treatment

Dampen a sponge or cloth with full strength apple cider vinegar and place it over a heat or air conditioning register. Allow air to circulate through the vinegar-wet cloth for 15 to 20 minutes and the air will feel fresh and pure.

Emily's Favorite Kitchen Deodorizer

Keep a small pump spray bottle of water, with 2 tablespoons of white vinegar added to it, handy in the kitchen. Whenever odor is a problem, a few puffs into the air will neutralize it. An old pump hair spray bottle works well, because it puts out a fine, easily diffused mist. Use when cooking fish, cabbage, after boilovers, or anytime the air needs a quick freshening.

Coffee Pots

Coffee oils are very thick and sticky, so they tend to collect on the inside of pots and on percolator parts. When they become old, these oils decompose. This releases the acids that give coffee a sour taste and rancid smell.

An occasional touch of vinegar will dissolve coffee oils and so keep coffee pots from developing rancid odors. Just add 1 tablespoon of vinegar to a full pot of hot water and let it set for 10 minutes. Rinse well and the pot will make excellent coffee again.

For heavy buildups, make this special pot of 'coffee' - replace coffee grounds with 1 teaspoon liquid detergent and 1 tablespoon vinegar. When the full brewing cycle has finished, rinse the pot several times with hot water.

Coffee Pot Cleaner

Mix together equal parts water and white vinegar and use only this for a complete cycle of an automatic coffee pot. It will freshen the pot, help to loosen and remove mineral deposits, and prevent build-up of rancid coffee oils. Great for soaking teapots, too!

Thermos Cleaner

Fill a stained vacuum bottle with a mixture made of 2 parts white vinegar to 1 part cold water. Let stand for an hour, then add a tablespoon of uncooked rice and shake for several minutes. Rinse several times and wipe dry.

Teapots need cleaned, too!

Kitchen Counter Tops

To preserve glossy surfaces, use vinegar and water to wipe down lightly soiled counter tops. Use detergent, soap or ammonia based products only when really needed, as they break down wax-based polishes. Laminated plastic counter tops (such as Formica) need to be kept covered with a layer of wax to protect them from tiny cuts and scratches which will eventually make the surface look dull.

Counter Top Scrubber

Make a great, disposable, counter top scrubber by dipping a piece of old nylon hose in vinegar and using it to scrub globs of stuck-on goo off laminated plastic counter tops. This combination has enough cleaning power to remove the mess, yet will not scratch the surface. (Really hard globs can be allowed to soak for a few minutes.)

Very Dirty Counter Tops

When counter tops have really hard globs of foods or other materials on them, use a vinegar compress to loosen the dirt. Soaking the material loose will save the work of scrubbing and scraping and, more importantly, save wear and tear on the counter top.

Wet a cloth, paper towel or sponge with full strength white vinegar. Lay it on the material to be loosened and let it soak for at least an hour. Wipe off as much of the dirt as possible and repeat as necessary.

Crumb Catcher

A cloth dampened with a light spray of vinegar will catch a whole counter top of crumbs, without spreading them all over.

Counter and Appliance Stain Remover

Mix a solution of equal parts white vinegar and water. Use a cloth or sponge wrung out of this fresh smelling mixture to wipe down appliances and counter tops. It will not leave streaks, and they will shine.

Copper Cleaner

1	cup white vinegar	1/4	cup flour
1/2	cup water	1/2	cup salt
1/2	cup powdered detergent		

Whisk all ingredients together, then slowly heat in a double boiler until the detergent is dissolved and the mixture begins to thicken. Set aside until cool. To use, wipe onto copper with a small cloth, let set for 30 seconds, then wipe off with a clean cloth.

Drain Cleaner

Slow-running drains can often be improved by treating them with baking soda and vinegar. Begin by sprinkling 1/4 cup soda into the drain. Immediately pour 1/2 cup vinegar into the drain. Allow it to foam and sizzle for a few minutes. When the action has stopped, pour at least 2 quarts of boiling water down the drain.

Drain & Septic Treatment

Plumbing lines which empty into septic systems can benefit from an occasional bacteria boosting treatment. Begin by using a vinegar and baking soda drain cleaner (see above) in all drains. When the drains are clean and free-running, pour 1 package dry yeast and 2/3 cup brown sugar into the toilet and flush twice. Do this about once a month and the system will work efficiently for years.

Drain Deodorizer

Pour 1/2 cup vinegar down each drain, every week. The vinegar will keep the drains smelling sweet (and discourage clogs, too)!

Magic Garbage Disposer Freshener

Mix equal parts apple cider vinegar and water and freeze the mixture in an ice cube tray. Store the frozen cubes in a plastic bag. Then, grind a few of these special freshener cubes in the disposer each week for instant cleaning that will also leave it smelling fresh.

Vinegar Magic For Aluminum Pots and Pans

Aluminum pans become discolored if they get a lot of exposure to salty foods, ammonia or cleaning products that contain ammonia. If 1/2 cup white vinegar, with a couple of cups of water added to it, is occasionally boiled in such pans, staining will be kept to a minimum.

For lightly stained cookware: make a paste of white vinegar and baking soda. Spread over stained aluminum cooking utensils. Remove with fine superfine steel wool.

For medium stains: mix the baking soda with an equal amount of cream of tartar, then stir in the vinegar.

For badly stained pans: use baking soda and cream of tartar (as for medium stains) and mix with vinegar which has been mixed half and half with liquid detergent.

Iron forms rust; copper forms verdigris.

Copper Pans

When copper pans oxidize, a green film forms. This is called verdigris and, while it is a bit unsightly on the outside of pans, it helps them do a better job of absorbing heat.

On the inside of pans this green oxide is a bigger problem - it is poisonous. This is why most pans only use copper on the outside, or sandwiched between two other metals. If a copper pan develops these patches of green on the inside, consider throwing it away. To clean verdigris from the inside of copper pans: fill with water, add 1/3 cup vinegar and 1/3 cup salt. Boil for 10 minutes and scrub vigorously. Rinse well.

No-Stick Pans

Mineral salts from hard water can build up on the surfaces of pans coated with fluorocarbon compounds. These no-stick coatings should not be scrubbed with harsh chemicals or steel wool pads. Whitish mineral stains can be removed by boiling 2 cups of water and 1/3 cup white vinegar in the pan for a few minutes, then wiping the pan dry with a soft cloth.

Foil & Vinegar Scrubbers

Make your own scrubber for removing cooked on food from pans and baking dishes. Simply crumple up a wad of aluminum foil (new or used), dip it in vinegar, and rub the cooked on food away. Extra hard spots can be soaked in vinegar for a few minutes before scrubbing.

Vinegar & Apple Cleaner

Remove stains from the inside of aluminum cookware by boiling 1 quart of water, 1/2 cup white vinegar and 1 cup apple peels for 15 minutes. (Also very good for removing the smell of cooking fish from the kitchen.)

Rust Stains From Metal

Rust stains on stainless steel sinks can be wiped away by scouring with salt, dampened with vinegar.

Never use an ammonia containing solution with one which contains bleach (or chlorine-based cleaners).

'Teflon' & 'Silver-stone' are two brand names for no-stick cookware.

Chapter Four

In The Bathroom, Bedroom & Office

Bathrooms are always a special cleaning challenge. They sprout mildew and mold, attract odors and breed tub and shower slime. Bedrooms are a haven for dust balls, stale air and musty smelling closets. Offices present their own problems with assorted chemical stains and paper bits. Vinegar can help solve all these problems.

BATHROOM

Better Wet Wipes

Mix 1 cup vinegar, 1 cup water and 1 tablespoon liquid detergent in a bowl. Wet small pieces of clean, soft cloth in the vinegar mixture, then wring them out. Place the cloths in a tightly capped container.

Use wet wipes for cleaning and moving spots on faucets and fixture handles, drains, around tub enclosures and sinks, and even on the outside surfaces of toilets. They also do a good job cleaning windows, walls and floors.

Disposable Wet Wipes

Make disposable wet wipes by substituting sheets of extra heavy paper towels for pieces of cloth. They are great for wiping up unpleasant bathroom messes.

Mildew

That slimy growth in showers, around tubs and in other damp places is really a plant. It is a soft, spongy fungus, and can be white as well as black or purplish in color. Mildew grows best where it is dark and the air is warm and wet and stagnant. It thrives in showers and tubs, where it lives on body oil, dirt particles and soap scum.

Vinegar helps to remove the dirt, oil and soap that provide its food. It also leaves behind an acid environment to slow the future growth of mildew.

Dryrot and corn smut are also fungus.

27

So, the cure for any area attacked by mildew, mold or other fungus is to keep it dry, give it lots of sunshine, and regularly rinse it with vinegar!

Mildew And Mold Removal

The metal edges of shower and tub surrounds are especially attractive to mold and mildew. Scrub them down with a piece of crumbled up foil which has been dipped in full strength vinegar. Use a toothbrush dipped in vinegar for crevices and corners. Rinse with clear water, then with water and vinegar and buff dry.

Use white vinegar to dissolve soap film and kill mold and mildew. It will leave the bathroom smelling fresh and clean. Use apple cider vinegar for the same cleaning power, but with a stronger, fresher, longer lasting fragrance.

Soap Film Remover

Shower walls, in particular, seem to attract scummy soap film. Vinegar and baking soda can eat right through it! Simply take 1 cup baking soda and add enough white vinegar to make a thick, frothy cream. Spread it over areas where soap film has built up and let set for 5 minutes. Wipe off with a soft brush or sponge, rinse in water with some white vinegar added to it and buff dry.

Extra Power Soap Film Treatment

Mix together 1/4 cup white vinegar and 1/4 cup ammonia.* Add enough baking soda to make a thick paste. Spread this mixture over the area that has a coating of soap film. Let set for 10 minutes, then remove with a medium-bristled brush. Follow with a rinse of cool water, with a little vinegar in it.

Soap Film Preventive

Prevent soap film buildup by rinsing all exposed surfaces, every week, with a solution of vinegar and water. A cup of white vinegar to a quart of water is about right for hard water areas, a cup to a gallon of water for soft water areas.

Bathroom Odors

Instead of using an aerosol air freshener to fight bathroom odors, keep a pump spray bottle of vinegar water handy. Just fill the bottle with water and 1 tablespoon white vinegar. Whenever odor relief is needed, a few sprays will release a fine mist that neutralizes odors.

For best results, use a pump sprayer of the type hair spray comes in. It will release a very fine mist, spreading the vinegar into the air rapidly.

A mist with vinegar in it, instead of a floral scent, is especially good for households where someone has hay fever or is allergic to flowers and grasses. Vinegar neutralizes odors without adding a fragrance that can trigger allergies and add to indoor pollution.

Hair In The Sink

Cleaning pesky hair clippings from the sink can be a messy, frustrating job. Make it easy with a dash of vinegar. Simply spray vinegar on a piece of bathroom tissue and use it to wipe out the sink. Fold the tissue over the hair, wipe again, discard the tissue and hair.

Denture Cleaner and Freshener

A quick brushing with white vinegar will help to brighten dentures. It will also remove lingering odors. If dentures are set overnight in water, adding 1/2 teaspoon vinegar will help keep them odor free.

Using apple cider vinegar will add a refreshing flavor to the mouth. Herbal vinegars, such as thyme or mint, also act as breath fresheners.

Ceramic Tile

Floors, back splashes, shower walls and such will shine their best if rinsed in a mild vinegar and water solution, then buffed dry. Keep ceramic tile showers free of soap scum and hard water salts buildup by drying after each use.

A synthetic chamois cloth does a wonderful job of wiping down tile because it absorbs water so well. Keep the cloth fresh and clean by washing it occasionally in a mild liquid detergent, then rinsing it in vinegar to neutralize the soap and minerals it will be constantly wiping up.

Hair Rollers, Brushes & Combs

Over time, hair rollers, brushes and combs pick up a coating of hair spray, mousse and setting gels. This buildup attracts dirt and dust, turning it into a dark, sticky coating. Remove this coating by soaking rollers, brushes and combs for an hour in a quart of warm water with a cup of white vinegar added to it. Then scrub with an old toothbrush which has been dipped in liquid detergent. The buildup will now come off easily. Follow with a clear water rinse, then a rinse in warm water with a dash of white vinegar. Blot most of the water off and air dry, in the sun if possible.

Shower Heads

When heavy mineral deposits are visible on the shower head, it usually means these salts have been deposited inside, too. Unscrew the fixture and soak it in full strength white vinegar. The vinegar will dissolve and soften the buildup. If the small openings are clogged, use a toothpick or small nail to remove the minerals which have been deposited on them. Then scrub with an old toothbrush and rinse well.

Keep shower heads sparkling bright by wiping them down once a week with white vinegar. Give the tiny nozzle openings special attention, so that mineral precipitations do not develop. A thin coating of wax can help prevent hard water deposits from sticking to the metal.

Shower Curtains

A shower curtain that is stained with mildew or mold can be revived by soaking it in a laundry tub of warm water with 2 cups of white vinegar added to it. Let it soak for a couple of hours (or over night) and then wash in warm, sudsy water and dry in the sun.

Wipe down the shower curtain on a regular basis with white vinegar and it will be less likely to develop mildew or mold stains. Just spray the bottom fourth of the curtain with white vinegar and wipe it off with a soft cloth.

Keep It Shiny

After wiping chrome, brass or other metal bathroom fixtures with vinegar and water, dry completely and apply two light coats of wax. They will look bright and shiny longer, clean up easier next time, and will resist the buildup of hard water mineral salts.

BEDROOM

Urine Stained Mattresses

Spray stains with white vinegar and blot dry. The process may need to be repeated several times, but it will lift stains and remove unpleasant odors.

Freshen Bedding

Musty, stale smelling blankets and bedspreads can be freshened, often without actually having to clean or wash them. Simply put the bedding in a clothes dryer with a cloth wrung out of full strength apple cider vinegar. With the dryer set to 'air,' let it fluff for 5 minutes. Most odors and dust will disappear, and the apple cider vinegar will leave a clean, outdoorsy smell behind. Dusty drapes can be refreshed in the same manner.

OFFICE

Taking The White Out

White correction fluid is wonderful stuff, until it shows up where it is not needed! Usually, a quick dab of white vinegar will melt it away. (For stubborn spots, reapply or soak for a few minutes.)

Super-Glued Fingers

When an errant drop of one of those new fast drying contact glues gets on skin, fingers can end up cemented together. For a skin saving remedy, soak in full strength vinegar.

Colored Paper Stains

Vivid shades of construction paper can brighten up office projects, but a little dampness can cause bright colors to transfer onto clothing. Lift these stains by dampening with a solution of half white vinegar, half water, then blot dry. Repeat until all trace of color is gone.

Books

After awhile, even the nicest books can develop a musty smell. Keep them spotlessly clean by running a vacuum cleaner over them frequently. If individual volumes need to be hand dusted, try wiping the covers with a soft cloth which has been very lightly sprayed with a weak vinegar and water solution. (You only want enough vinegar to kill the musty smell and to deter mold and fungus growth.)

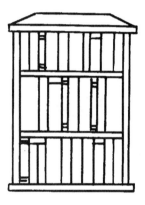

Bookshelves

Use a strong solution of vinegar and sudsy water to wipe off bookshelves, then rinse in clear water and dry. Make shelf cleaning less exhausting by only removing 4 or 5 books from a shelf. Wash and dry the exposed part of the shelf, then slide the next 4 or 5 books over this clean spot and wash the part now exposed.

Repeat the process to the end of the shelf. When the entire shelf has been washed and dried, slide the books back to their original positions and replace the few books which were removed at the beginning. This way, lifting of heavy books is minimized for the one doing the cleaning, shelf order is maintained, and the books do not suffer unnecessary handling.

Chapter Five

Vinegar Goes Outside

Vinegar is exceptionally useful in the garden, yard and garage. For cleaning and polishing, or for deterring insects, it is difficult to find a better, more environmentally safe substance.

Vinegar is a gentle, inexpensive cleaner, yet it is surprisingly effective. It is safe for children and pets, yet it attacks germs and harmful bacteria. Whether shining and polishing the car or washing the dog, there is usually a good a reason to keep the vinegar bottle handy!

GARDEN

Gardener's Friend
Keep ants away from plants by making a circle around them with vinegar. Just dribble a generous stream around each plant. It will act as a barrier to wandering ants.

Home Ant Repellant
Sprinkle apple cider vinegar on windowsills, around doors and other openings to prevent ants from entering the home.

Flowerpots
After a very short time, clay flowerpots develop a buildup of mineral salts. This whitish buildup not only looks ugly, it interferes with the way the pot should breathe and absorb water. Remove mineral salts by rubbing with a scrub brush dipped in full strength vinegar. Finish with a clear water rinse.

Soil Ph Balancer
Many plants need an acid soil environment to thrive. To acidify alkaline ground, pour 1 cup vinegar into a bucket of water and dribble it in a circle around acid loving plants such as azaleas, blueberries, marigolds, and radishes.

YARD & GARAGE

Barbecue Grills

Place soiled racks from barbecue grills in a large black plastic bag. Use 2 cups vinegar to wet them down, then tie a loose knot in the bag to seal in the moisture. Lay the plastic bag in the sun for 3 to 4 hours, then add 2 tablespoons dishwasher detergent and 2 quarts hot water to it. Re-tie the bag and allow it to soak in the sun for another 2 hours. Burnt food and stains will now wipe off easily.

Cement Garage Floors

Sweeping cement can produce a fine dust that is very corrosive. Reduce dust with newspapers and vinegar water. To a gallon of water, add 1 cup vinegar. Sprinkle this liberally over a pile of shredded newspapers. Toss the shredded newspapers over the floor, then sweep as usual. Dust will cling to the damp newspaper and the vinegar will help neutralize odors.

Green Sweep For Cement Floors

Cut down on dust when sweeping cement floors by spreading grass clippings over the floor (the fresher the better). Dampen the clippings by sprinkling with water that has had a little apple cider vinegar added to it. The sweeping will not generate dust, and when the job is done, the area will smell fresh and clean!

CAR & BOAT

Odor-Eater For Car Ashtrays

Wipe ashtrays out with a wadded up newspaper or paper towel moistened with full strength vinegar. Allow to air dry. The vinegar will neutralize ashtray odor, and as it drys it will remove stale smells from the entire car.

No-Freeze, No-Streak Windshield Washer Liquid

    1/2   cup white vinegar
    2   cups rubbing alcohol
    2   teaspoons liquid detergent
    6   cups water

Stir the detergent in the water and when it is well mixed, add the vinegar and alcohol. This liquid will also help remove ice and snow from a cold car's windshield. Simply spray a good coating on before trying to clear the windshield of ice. It will make the job much easier.

Car Chrome Cleaner

Remove small spots of rust from car chrome by rubbing them out with a piece of aluminum foil dipped in vinegar. Rinse, and then finish up with a coat of wax to discourage new spots from forming.

Decal Remover

Soak bumper decals in full strength white vinegar and they will come off easily. Just wrap a cloth around the bumper, wet it thoroughly with vinegar, then allow it to set for 45 minutes. The glue holding the decal to the bumper should begin to break down, making removal much easier!

Boat Cleaning

Aluminum boats, in particular, are very sensitive to alkalines in water. These salts can etch aluminum and cause it to discolor. Vinegar neutralizes alkalines, so it can be used to scrub off discoloration. Use full strength white vinegar to scrub stains, but always follow with a clear water rinse, then immediately wipe dry.

ESPECIALLY FOR CAMPERS

No-Scrub Laundry

Do laundry while on the road by placing soiled clothes in a watertight container with a tiny bit of detergent and some white vinegar. After a few hours on the road the laundry will be ready to rinse and hang out to dry!

Vacation Skin

Always tuck a bottle of vinegar into the camping pack. It is great for soothing skin that has been subjected to sun and wind. It is also good for softening hard water.

Iron Pans And Kettles

Half the fun of camp cooking is using a big old iron frying pan or kettle. A dash of vinegar added to the cooking pot will help transfer iron from these utensils to food.

Fiberglass Campers

Because it is light in weight, many camping trailers use fiberglass for both exterior and interior surfaces. This material tends to pickup hard water stains and soap scum film. White vinegar helps dissolve this whitish discoloration. Use it on fiberglass sinks, wall panels, tubs and showers.

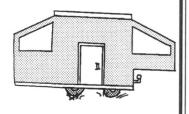

Plastic Picnic Coolers

Spray a strong vinegar and detergent solution over the inside o' cooler. Close it up to soak while you wash the outside of the coole vinegar and water. By the time you get to the inside, odors and food will wipe right off.

Chapter Six

PETS

Itch Control For Dogs

Help to control itching by following the dog's bath with a vinegar and water rinse. Add 1/3 cup apple cider vinegar to 2 quarts water and pour over a well shampooed and rinsed dog. Do not rinse out. Dry as usual and the coat should be soft and shiny, and there should be much less itching and scratching.

Odor Control

Control odor from any furry pet by spraying its coat daily with mild vinegar water. 1 tablespoon to a cup of water is about right for eliminating odors.

Behavior Control

Train cats and dogs to respect furniture with a squirt gun filled with water which has a teaspoon of vinegar added to it. Whenever the pet approaches a forbidden area, tell them 'No' and reinforce it with a quick liquid reminder. Soon, simply picking up the squirt gun will ensure good behavior.

Carpet Spots

Use a solution made of 1 cup white vinegar to a gallon of lukewarm water to neutralize urine stains in carpet. Sprinkle it on, then immediately blot it up. Repeat as needed.

Pet Hair

Turn an old tube sock inside out and slip in onto your hand. Spray it, lightly, with white vinegar and use it to wipe down your pet. Loose hair will stick to the damp sock. Great for cats, dogs, hampsters, rabbits and other furry creatures. It also deodorizes their fur. A vinegar dampened sock is also good for removing pet hairs from furniture, carpets and clothing.

Vinegar Is For Birds, Too!

Keep birdbaths clean by rinsing them out regularly. A few drops of vinegar added to birdbath water will help control the growth of fungus and bacteria.

inegar Is
or People

Over the years vinegar has been credited with to power to act as a soothing skin tonic, add shining highlights to hair and, when combined with herbs, bring calming comfort or energizing zest to the bath.

What follows is a collection of old-fashioned remedies which use vinegar to make people feel better. Please remember, these old-time remedies are not medically proven. They are simply ways many people have used vinegar mixtures for relief of discomfort and for its fresh, pleasing aroma.

EVERYONE

Instantly Soft Hands

Pour 1/2 cup water, with 1 teaspoon vinegar stirred in, over the hands. Sprinkle the water and vinegar dampened hands with 1/2 teaspoon white sugar, then with 1 teaspoon baby oil. Work this mixture into the hands for 2 minutes, then wash with a gentle soap. Hands will be almost magically smooth and velvety feeling!

Silky Smooth Hands

Make hands silky smooth, and keep them that way, by moisturizing them in warm water and vinegar, then sealing the moisture in with petroleum jelly. For best results, treat hands just before retiring for the night.

Add 1 tablespoon apple cider vinegar to 2 cups warm water. Soak hands in this mixture for 5 minutes, then pat them dry. Smooth 1/2 teaspoon petroleum jelly over the hands and pull on a pair of cotton gloves. By morning the hands will be unbelievably soft and smooth, no matter how much hard work they do during the day.

Soft Feet

Rough skin on the feet can be softened by soaking them in water and vinegar, then applying body lotion. Use lukewarm water, with a tablespoon of apple cider vinegar added for each quart of water. Pat the feet completely dry, gently apply body lotion, then cover with cotton socks.

Softer Feet

Hard, dry calluses and coarse skin can make feet feel uncomfortable, and contribute to pain when walking. Soften feet by soaking for 5 minutes in warm water with a little vinegar in it, then rubbing granulated white sugar over rough spots. Follow with a quick baby oil massage, then wash thoroughly with a gentle soap before covering with cotton socks. (Baby oil makes feet VERY slippery! Always wash it all off BEFORE standing or walking.)

One way to prevent slipping is to soak feet in vinegar and water, in the bathtub. Then, fill the tub for a regular bath (let the vinegar do double duty as a soothing, full body conditioner). Use the sugar and baby oil while sitting in the tub. This way there is no mess, and no chance of falling!

Soften Corns & Calluses

To soften skin made rough and scaly by corns and callouses, soak the feet every day in a pan of warm soapy water, to which a cup of vinegar has been added.

Easier Nail Trimming

If tough toenails make trimming them a chore, soak the feet in warm water with a couple of tablespoons of vinegar added to it. After about 10 minutes, nails will be much softer and easier to trim.

Dandruff Remedy

Shampoo and rinse the hair as usual, then work a solution made of equal parts apple cider vinegar and water through the hair. Do not rinse this out.

Grandmother's Dandruff Treatment

After washing and rinsing the hair as usual, treat it to 5 minutes of conditioning with a mixture of 1/2 cup apple cider vinegar to which 2 aspirins have been added. Rinse well, then follow with a final conditioning rinse of a quart of warm water to which 1/2 cup apple cider vinegar has been added.

Herbal Baths

Homemade scented vinegars are the essential component of great herbal baths. Use 1/4 to 1/2 cup vinegar to a tub of warm water. For a relaxing soak, use herbal vinegars such as catnip, lemon balm, lavender, borage, chamomile or slippery elm. For an invigorating soak, use herbal vinegars such as ginger, peppermint, sage, or tarragon.

Steamy Vinegar Facials

Heat 1 cup herbal vinegar to the boiling point and pour it into a large bowl. Lean over the bowl and drape a towel over your head and the bowl. Allow the warm, moist steam to soften facial skin. When the vinegar has cooled, pat it onto the face as a cleansing astringent. Strawberry vinegar is especially good for the skin.

An herbal vinegar steam treatment is a wonderful way to soften the skin before applying a moisturizer, or to soothe the skin after a cleansing facial.

ESPECIALLY FOR WOMEN

Vinegar Facial Mask
1/4 cup oatmeal
1 tablespoon honey
1 tablespoon apple cider vinegar

Combine ingredients and pat the mixture onto wet skin. Let set until dry. Wash off with cool water and apply moisturizer.

Bubble Bath

Put 1 cup vegetable oil in a bottle and add 1/4 cup apple cider vinegar and 2 tablespoons liquid hand soap. Shake well before adding a few cupfuls to bath water. A few drops of perfume may be added, if desired. Or, replace the apple cider vinegar with lavender, rosemary or woodruff herbal vinegar.

Hair Moisturizer.
1 egg yolk
1 teaspoon honey
1/4 cup olive oil
1/4 cup apple cider vinegar

Beat all ingredients together for several minutes, or combine in a blender to produce a thick, smooth cream. Rub the mixture into the hair and onto the scalp and let set for about 10 minutes. Shampoo out and rinse in lukewarm water with a splash of apple cider vinegar added to it.

Skin Lightening Solution

1/4	cup white vinegar
1/4	cup lemon juice
1	cup white wine
1	tablespoon honey

Put all ingredients into a jar and shake until will mixed. Pat onto the skin morning and evening.

Shiny Hair Spray

Combine 1 cup water and 1/4 cup apple cider vinegar in a pump-spray bottle. A light spritz will add sparkling highlights and a bit of body to dull, limp hair. It works even better with a drop or two of perfume added to it, or if the apple cider vinegar is replaced with herbal vinegar.

Oil & Vinegar Hair Treatment

Restore the health of dry, sun damaged hair with oil and vinegar! Heat 1/4 cup olive oil until it is comfortably warm, then massage it into the scalp and hair. Make sure ends get a good coating, using extra oil for long hair.

Next, add 1/2 cup apple cider vinegar to a sink full of very hot water. Soak a towel in the hot vinegar water and then wring it out. Wrap the warm, wet towel around the olive oil treated hair and cover with a second, dry towel. After 15 minutes, remove both towels and wash the hair with a gentle shampoo.

Soft Skin - Forever

Keep the skin on your face soft and youthful looking by moisturizing it before applying makeup. Just wring a washcloth out of warm water with a dash of vinegar in it. Hold the warm, wet washcloth over the face for 15 - 20 seconds, pat the skin barely dry, then apply moisturizer, followed by makeup. Skin will remain soft and youthful looking, and will be less likely to develop blemishes.

ESPECIALLY FOR MEN

Men's Scented Splash-On

Vinegar with spices and herbs added to it was the original skin tonic for men. Some of the best ones for tightening and conditioning the skin are made with spearmint, bee balm, chamomile or blackberry leaves.*

See chapter on cooking with vinegar for herbal vinegars.

Skin Bracer

For a healing, refreshing facial tonic, mix 1/2 teaspoon cream of tartar and two tablespoons vinegar into a half cup of warm water. Pat onto the face after washing.

Begin by mixing together a basic aftershave lotion of 1 cup white vinegar and 2 tablespoons sweet clover honey. Add 1 tablespoon of an aromatic herb. Let the preparation set for a week, strain out the herb leaves, and the aftershave lotion is ready to use!

Some especially fragrant herbs for aftershave lotions are sage, thyme, cloves, bay and coriander. Combine a couple of herbs to make your own distinctive scent.

Another Aftershave

Combine 1/2 cup white vinegar, 1/2 cup vodka and 2 tablespoons honey. Variations:

• Spice it up by soaking 1 teaspoon aromatic herbs in the mixture for about a month, then strain and use.

• Apple cider vinegar, substituted for the white vinegar, makes a more robust aftershave

• Rubbing alcohol may be substituted for the vodka for a less expensive version.

• A teaspoon of glycerin added to the aftershave mixture will soothe and moisturize a dry face.

Refrigerated Aftershave

This is a cooling aftershave for warm weather use. Puree a small cucumber in the blender (do not peel) with several fresh mint leaves. Add this mixture to a basic aftershave and set in the refrigerator overnight. Strain and it is ready to use. (Must be kept refrigerated.)

BABY, TOO!

Baby Bottle Nipples

When boiling nipples to sterilize them, add a teaspoon of vinegar to each 2 cups of water. It will help prevent them developing an 'off' taste. (For fast sterilizing, try boiling the nipples and vinegar water in the microwave.)

Diaper Rash

Discourage rashes on baby's bottom by adding 3/4 cup white vinegar to the last rinse water for diapers. (Diapers should always be rinsed twice.) Skip the fabric softener when drying diapers. Chemicals in softeners may irritate baby's delicate skin, and softeners make diapers less able to soak up liquids quickly!

Easy Highchair Cleaning

Wash baby's highchair quickly and easily in the shower. Simply set the chair in the shower, spray with full strength white vinegar and let set for 3 minutes. Then turn the shower on for another 3 minutes. A quick buffing with a brush will now loosen any dried on food, then another quick rinse will complete the job. The chair will be shiny clean, with no hard scrubbing or scraping.

Do not soak wooden chairs!

Baby Odors

Save on utilities, neutralize odors, humidify, and safety-proof baby's room with one simple trick! Take a damp towel, direct from the washing machine, and spray it with white vinegar. Hang the towel over the top of the door to baby's room. As the towel dries it will control odors, add moisture to the air, and prevent the door from closing all the way, so the little one cannot accidently lock his or her self in the room.

Sanitizing Toys

Wipe down plastic dolls, blocks, cars and other toys with a cloth wrung out of a solution made of 1 part vinegar and 4 parts water. Or, spray full strength white vinegar onto a damp cloth and use it to wipe dirt and germs from toys.

Chapter Seven

Vinegar & Laundry

3000 B.C. — Cotton fabric is first made in the Indus valley.

400 B.C. — Generally, laundry is washed in a stream.

1625 — Soap is made at home by boiling grease, fat and wood ashes.

1837 — Procter & Gamble starts selling soap.

1907 — Thor, the first completely self-contained electric washing machine is introduced by Hurley Machine Company of Chicago.

1907 — Persil, the first dishwashing detergent, comes on the market. (Unfortunately, it is not suitable for heavy duty laundry use.)

1922 — Maytag's Gyrofoam washing machine is a market star.

1934 — The first Washeteria (laundromat) opens in Fort Worth, Texas with four washing machines.

1946 — Tide, the first detergent strong enough for washing clothes is introduced by Procter & Gamble.

A popular homemaker's advice book of 1849 admonished the housekeeper: "Remove soil spots with equal parts vinegar, turpentine and linseed oil." And, "Boil soiled laundry for 20 minutes in water with soap, lye, sal soda, and turpentine."

Wash day has changed! Today's fabrics are often delicate, and require gentle cleaning. As the washing of clothes left river banks and soap gave way to detergent, standards of cleanliness changed, too. Now, laundry is expected to be more than clean. Whites must gleam and colors need to sparkle.

Fabrics which come through the laundry room may be synthetic or natural, delicate or sturdy, drab or iridescent, easily faded or colorfast. This parade of materials, textures, fibers and dyes presents difficult cleaning choices — does one use soap or detergent? Bleach, an alkaline washing booster or vinegar?

Understanding how laundry cleaning substances do their jobs can help you decide when to use soap, when to use detergent and when to use vinegar as a cleaning agent.

SOAP OR DETERGENT?

Soaps clean by encouraging tiny bits dirt to become solid curds that can be rinsed out by water. Soap leaves a light, oily film behind that protects wood, but attracts more dirt to fabrics.

Detergents include an ingredient to make water 'wet' better, by breaking its surface tension. This lets it do a better job of dissolving dirt out of fabrics. Detergents also contain emulsifiers, which help to keep the bits of dirt suspended in water. Rinsing in lots of water helps get rid of this dirt, too.

Most soaps and detergents are alkaline. Vinegar's acid nature makes it a good neutralizing rinse for laundry washed in either soap or detergent.

USE VINEGAR WITH CARE

Vinegar has been considered, throughout history, to be an indispensable part of cleaning laundry. This is because it is often the best product for rinsing natural fibers. It is not always as compatible with synthetic fibers.

There are some fabrics for which vinegar is not appropriate. For example, in some situations vinegar acts as a mild bleaching agent. So, before applying it to dark or bright colors, test it on small, hidden areas. And, because vinegar is an acid, it can intensify the actions of other acids, making it a poor choice for treating some man-made fibers.

Generally, silk and wool can take a dash of full strength white vinegar. For fine cottons and linens, use vinegar which has been diluted with an equal amount of water, as it can weaken these fibers.

Acetate and triacetate are cellulose based and should not be exposed to vinegar at all. Triacetate is the material which is often used for lightweight, finely pleated skirts. Ramie, a plant fiber based material, is not helped by vinegar either. (When cellulose products decompose they turn into something much like vinegar!)

Surface tension is what lets a water spider 'walk on water!'

USE VINEGAR TO NEUTRALIZE ALKALINES

Vinegar is particularly good at neutralizing alkaline stains. So, use vinegar to neutralize the effects of caustic products, such as dishwasher detergents, and solutions containing lye, such as oven cleaners.

This means vinegar can be very helpful as a neutralizing rinse for hands exposed to caustic alkaline cleaners. And, use vinegar on stains made by:

Syrup	Food Dye	Apples	Blueberries
Jelly	Hair Colorings	Pears	Grapefruit
Honey	Spaghetti	Cherries	Blackberries
Oranges	Perfume	Grapes	Raspberries

Vinegar is useful for removing many of the discolorations caused by medicines, inks and fabric dyes. It is also good for lifting traces of beer, wine, grass, soft drinks, coffee, tea and tobacco.

Ammonia is very alkaline, and can alter the color of some dyes. Stop this change in color by neutralizing the action of ammonia with vinegar. When fabric begins to bleed color because it has been exposed to ammonia, rinse it in cool water. Follow with a strong vinegar and water solution, then finish with a clear water rinse.

One of the few stains vinegar should not be used on, is one caused by blood. Vinegar can set it and make it nearly impossible to get out. (See Spit & Polish, near the end of this chapter, for vinegar's contribution to removing blood stains.) Do not use vinegar on stains made by: blood, vomit, eggs, butter, milk or grease.

LAUNDRY HINTS

Pre-Treating Solution
4 Tablespoons white vinegar   2 Tablespoons baking soda
3 Tablespoons ammonia   Cool water
1 Tablespoon liquid detergent

Many laundry stains many be removed by pre-treating clothes with a few spritzes of this stain remover. To make, put the vinegar, ammonia, and liquid detergent in a quart-size pump spray bottle. Mix together, then add the baking soda. When it stops foaming, fill the bottle with cool water and use immediately. (If the mixture is stored in this container, the pump spray may be damaged.)

General Perspiration Stains

White vinegar is the traditional remedy for removing perspiration stains from clothes. Sturdy fabrics can be treated with a full strength application of vinegar, rubbed in as they are put in the washing machine. Delicate fabrics should be soaked in vinegar diluted half and half with water.

Stubborn Perspiration Stains

White fabric that has been stained by perspiration can sometimes be cleaned with white vinegar, salt and lots of sunlight. Begin by wringing the entire garment out in cool water. Then soak the stains with full strength white vinegar. Spread the clothing out in direct sunlight and then sprinkle the stain with salt. When the garment is completely dry, repeat the process. Most perspiration stains will eventually come out this way.

Perspiration and Silks

Delicate silk garments are notorious for attracting perspiration stains. White vinegar is the safest, surest way to pre-treat this kind of discoloration. Many silks can tolerate a brief splash of full strength white vinegar to underarm areas without harm. (As always, test on an inconspicuous area before using any stain treatment!)

To begin, wet the entire garment, then apply white vinegar to discolored underarm stains. Let set for 3 minutes (longer on sturdy, colorfast fabrics and some whites). Wash as usual, being sure to add a dash of white vinegar to the final rinse water.

Keep Silks Shiny

To help silk garments keep their soft shine, always include a dash of white vinegar in their last rinse water. It helps them retain their glossy sheen.

Easy White Vinegar Rinse

An easy way to add vinegar to the last rinse water is to soak several white washcloths in full strength white vinegar and store them in a closed container. Then, just toss one of these prepared cloths into the rinse water when the washer tub has filled. It saves measuring and eliminates the possibility of splashing vinegar directly onto delicate fabrics.

Static Cling Solution

Make your own dryer sheets by preparing several small cloths wrung out of full strength white vinegar (as above). Then, simply toss a damp cloth into the dryer with each load of laundry. (This is also a good way to freshen and soften clothes if you forget to add vinegar to the last rinse cycle!)

Tumble until just barely dry.

Static Cling

Fight static cling in the dryer with nylon fabric and vinegar. Simply spray a 2 foot square of nylon net with a half and half solution of white vinegar and water and add it to a dryer load of clothes. The nylon net square will not only help reduce static cling, it will collect lint.

Warmer Blankets

The fluff on the blanket is what makes it keep you warm. The softer and fluffier the blanket, the better job it will do of keeping you warm. Spray lots of white vinegar on blankets before drying them. It will help to make them soft and fluffy. (Or, add the vinegar to the rinse water.)

Ink Stains

Ink stains can often be lifted by soaking them in white vinegar. Put full strength vinegar on ink stains, allow to set for 15 seconds, then blot. Repeat several times for dark stains, then wash as usual.

Coffee Stains

Blot coffee splatters until as much as possible of the liquid is removed. Immediately rinse in cool water. Follow with a rinse of white vinegar, then wash in lukewarm, soapy water.

Tea Stains

Fresh stains can be treated as coffee stains. Dried tea (and coffee) stains should be soaked for 30 minutes in white vinegar before washing in warm, soapy water.

Stubborn Coffee and Tea Stains

Coffee or tea stains that are very dark, or those that have been allowed to set, require extra treatment. Dampen the stain with white vinegar and sprinkle it with salt. Then, expose the stain to bright sunlight for at least an hour. Follow this by washing the material as usual. Repeat the process as necessary.

Red Wine Stains

Blot spills thoroughly, then immediately rinse the area with white wine. Blot again, until nearly dry, then rinse several times with white vinegar. Wash with mild suds and check to see if any discoloration remains. If further treatment is needed, soak in vinegar, then wash again in soapy water before drying.

Alternate Red Wine Remover

Blot as much of the liquid up as possible, then saturate the stain with a solution made of 1 tablespoon white vinegar and 3 tablespoons water. Rub the discoloration with salt, set in the sun until dry. Repeat if needed.

Rust Stains

Rust marks on cloth can usually be lifted with white vinegar and salt. Simply wet the rust stain with vinegar and then cover it with salt. Let it dry, preferably in the sun. Rinse the salt out and reapply until the stain is gone.

Basic Fabric Softener

Add 1/3 cup white vinegar to the final rinse water for softer, scent-free laundry. This inexpensive laundry treatment is safe for the gentlest fabrics and is great for those who are allergic to harsh chemicals and strong scents.

Amazing Fabric Softener

Combine 1/3 cup white vinegar and 1/3 cup baking soda and add the mixture to the final rinse water for even softer laundry. This combination is scent-free and irritation-free, good for the most delicate skin and fabrics.

Softener Hint: Keep vinegar-based fabric softeners in a pump spray bottle, such as liquid hand soap comes in. Then just add a few squirts to laundry water. No muss, no fuss!

Scented Fabric Softener

To add a very faint hint of clean, outdoorsy smell to laundry, use apple cider in any of the previous fabric softeners. For stronger scents, use herbal vinegars.

Lint Trap

Hard water can cause a buildup of minerals on the lint trap of the washing machine. Soak it in full strength vinegar for a couple of hours, then use a brush to remove the deposits.

Panty Hose Revitalizer

Soak stretched out, shapeless panty hose in 1 quart of warm water, with 1/4 cup white vinegar added to it. Let them set for 5 minutes, then squeeze gently and blot with a bath towel. (Never wring or stretch wet hose.) Allow the panty hose to dry, spread out flat on a towel.

Brightener For Synthetics

When polyester or nylon fabrics have become dull and drab looking, they can sometimes be revitalized by boiling them in 2 quarts of water, with 3/4 cup white vinegar added to it.

Protecting Wool

Good wools, as well as silks, can be easily damaged by harsh alkaline laundry products. For many hundreds of years white vinegar has been the cleaning fluid of choice for these fabrics. It helps to keep them soft, while lifting odors and stains.

Help keep the fibers of wool garments springy and resilient by including a couple of tablespoons of white vinegar in the last rinse water. This will also protect colors by preventing a buildup of soap or detergent residues.

Renewing Wool Apparel
Add new life to wool garments whose cuffs, bottoms or necklines have become stretched out and have lost their ability to snap back into their original shape. Combine vinegar and heat to recondition these wool clothes.

Wool revitalizer: Add 2 tablespoons of white vinegar to a small bucket of very hot water. Carefully dip only the stretched out edge of the garment into the hot water. Immediately blot with a towel, then blow dry with a hair dryer set on its highest setting.

Alpaca
Alpaca is a wool-like fiber from llamas. This material will hold its shape and remain soft and springy for many years if rinsed in water with a tablespoon of white vinegar in it.

Camel Hair Wool
This is an exceptional soft and silky kind of wool. Wash it in gentle suds, rinse in a dilute water and vinegar solution, and dry on a flat surface.

Angora
Angora has a texture much like that of fine lamb's wool. It can be made from the fur of angora rabbits or goats. It responds well to a gentle washing, followed by a rinse in cool water with a couple of tablespoons of white vinegar mixed in.

Cashmere
This wool is named after the goat whose undercoat provides the hair it is made of. Originally found in Kashmir, Tibet, these goats are now raised in many other areas. Treat cashmere as any good wool.

Wool Mixes
Wool is animal hair, and sometimes it is almost as fine as fur. Most wool comes from sheep, but mixed wool can contain hair from goats, rabbits, llamas, etc. The finest wool is made from the light downy underfur of the animals. These short hairs produce an extra soft wool.

Mohair is another name for angora.

Fresh Smelling Linens

Remove stale odors from linens by spraying them, lightly, with vinegar water, then fluffing them in the dryer for 5 or 10 minutes. (To a 1 quart pump spray bottle of water, add 1 or 2 tablespoons of white vinegar.) Or, put the dry linens in the dryer with a vinegar and water dampened bath towel.

Easy Creases For Pants

'No-iron" cotton pants will hold a sharp crease if treated with wax and vinegar. Begin by turning the pants inside out. Then run the bottom of a wax candle down the crease line (on the wrong side of the fabric).

Next, turn the pants right side out and cover the crease line with a cloth wrung out of half water, half white vinegar. Press with a very hot iron until dry. The crease will be sharp, and it will stay that way for a long time!

Wrinkle Remover

Remove wrinkles from stored clothes by hanging them up in the bathroom. Put 1 cup vinegar in the bath tub and turn the hot water in the shower on. When the tub is 1/2 full, turn off the water and allow the clothes to hang in the steamy room for 20 minutes. Most wrinkles will be removed and any stale odors will be gone, too.

Scorched Ironing

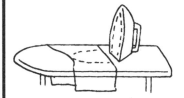

When a too-hot iron leaves an ugly spot of scorched fabric behind, a cloth damped with white vinegar will often remove the mark and save the day. Begin by wetting a clean, soft cloth with full strength white vinegar. Pat the vinegar onto the scorched spot, and let it set for a few minutes. If the scorch remains, wet it with vinegar once again. (Add a dash of salt for stubborn marks.)

Reviving Straw Hats

Stained and misshapen straw hats can be revived with a vinegar and salt treatment. Stir 1/2 cup salt into a large bucket or laundry tub of warm water. When the salt has dissolved, submerge the hat in the water.

When the straw is soft, gently wipe away any stains, using a little liquid soap if necessary. Remove the hat from the water and allow to drain for a few minutes. Gently push it into the desired shape, then spray the hat with a fine mist of vinegar water. (Add 1 teaspoon white vinegar to 1 cup water.) Allow to dry, away from the sun.

Crystal Clear Leather Cleaner

1/4	cup white vinegar	1	cup water
1/4	cup rubbing alcohol		

Gently wipe leather with a cloth dampened in clear leather cleaner, then dry at once with another cloth. This cleaner also works well on leather look-alike fabrics.

Curtains and Sheer Panels

Revitalize delicate fabric window coverings by using this vinegar based treatment in the final rinse. To a quart of hot water, add 1 tablespoon white vinegar and 2 envelopes of plain (unsweetened, unflavored) gelatin. Add this mixture to the final rinse water and dry as usual. Limp fabrics will be instantly revitalized!

Removing Gum

Break up sticky gum residue by soaking it in white vinegar. Begin by scraping away as much of the gum as possible. Then pat white vinegar onto what remains and let set for 20 minutes. Blot the vinegar away, taking as much of the gum with it as possible. Repeat until all the gum is gone.

Spit & Polish

For one of the best ways vinegar can help remove stains, it does not even need to touch the stain! Stains made by dairy products such as milk, eggs and cream are best dissolved by special digestive enzymes — the kind of enzymes found in human spit.

To lift these stains, place a few tablespoons of apple cider vinegar in a small bowl and breathe the vapor that rises from it. This will encourage digestive juices to flow, ensuring plenty of spit for soaking away stains. Small drops of blood or wine that have left spots on cloth can often be removed this way, and some kinds of grease, too.

Something Good Just Got Better

Ordinary white vinegar contains a 5% solution of acetic acid. A special just-for-cleaning white vinegar can contain a 10% solution of acetic acid. This 'super vinegar' will lift some stains faster, and it can make cleaning with vinegar better than ever!

PLEASE REMEMBER!

Always test fabrics and surfaces before using even a gentle cleaner like vinegar. No one cleaner is perfect for every laundry chore. Vinegar's antibacterial, antiseptic, and mild bleaching actions, as well as its acid nature may not be perfectly safe for every fabric. As with all cleaning substances, your own test on fabrics is the only sure test of safety.

The Heinz company makes just for cleaning white vinegar.

Chapter Eight

Cooking With Vinegar

Vinegar does more than just clean, it is one of the most ancient and useful foods. One reason vinegar is a safe basic ingredient for pickling, marinating and preserving is because it prevents the growth of botulism bacteria. And, at only two calories per tablespoon, it is the ideal topping for salads and vegetables.

Vinegar is well-known for its ability to tenderize meat and vegetables and to give foods robust flavor without added salt. It is an inexpensive way to turn dull vegetables into pickled delights and to pep up salads, sauces and dressings. A few ways to cook with vinegar follow:

Chef's Fish
After deep frying fish, spray each piece, while hot, with a mist of apple cider vinegar. It makes a tangy difference everyone will love and moderates fishy odors. Make strongly flavored fish taste milder by presoaking raw fish in 1 cup of water which has had 1/2 cup white vinegar added to it.

Better Hot Dogs
Improve the flavor of hot dogs by boiling them a few minutes in water with a tablespoon of vinegar added to it. They will taste better, and if you pierce them before boiling, they will be have less fat (and calories)!

Tangy Chinese Vegetable Dip
1/3	cup plum jelly	1/3	cup apple cider vinegar
1/3	cup applesauce	1/2	teaspoon brown sugar

Mix well, double the plum jelly for a more zesty sauce. Also good drizzled over fried noodles.

Salad Dressing
Personalize salad dressings by adding 1/4 cup herb flavored vinegar to commercial mayonnaise, or make oil and vinegar salad dressings with your own herbal vinegars.

Chicken Soup

Boil a cutup chicken in 2 quarts of water and 1/4 cup vinegar until the meat begins to fall off the bones. Strain the liquid and return 1 cup of chopped chicken to the soup pot. Add 1 minced onion, 2 tablespoons parsley, 5 cloves of garlic, 2 chopped stalks of celery, and 1 diced green pepper. Season with 1 teaspoon dill seeds, 1/4 teaspoon pepper and 1 tablespoon parsley. Simmer for 45 minutes and serve.

Fruit & Vinegar

Wash and mash fresh, well ripened fruit, using 2 cups of vinegar for each cup of fruit. Set in the refrigerator for 4 or 5 days. Strain off the flavored vinegar and heat it to the boiling point. Add 1/2 cup sugar for each cup of vinegar and simmer until the sugar is dissolved. Store in a glass jar.

Good fruits for making vinegar are: raspberries, blueberries, blackberries, strawberries and peaches. Combine several fruits for even better flavor. (Lemon and orange go well with most berries.) Plum is an exceptionally good vinegar. Drizzle it over a fresh fruit platter for a low calorie taste delight.

Vinegar Marinate

Begin with equal parts white vinegar and water. Add about 3 tablespoons of sugar and a dash of salt for each cup of vinegar. Use marinate to tenderize meats and vegetables, or to preserve beans, eggplant, broccoli and other vegetables. (Some examples of preserving vegetables follow.)

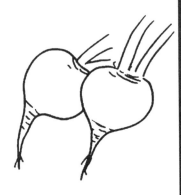

Vinegar & Onions

Wash tiny onions, peel, blanch, and cover with a layer of salt. Sit overnight and rinse the salt off. Add to enough Vinegar Marinate to cover and boil with spices until the onions are just barely tender (about 10 minutes). For a pound of onions use 1 tablespoon pickling spice, 4 cloves and 4 peppercorns.

Vinegar & Beets

Heat vinegar, water, sugar, and salt (as in Vinegar Marinate) to the boiling point, pour over sliced, fresh-cooked or canned beets. Marinate for at least 24 hours before serving.

Spicy Vegetables & Vinegar

Wash and cut vegetables into bite-sized pieces and blanch with a solution made of equal parts vinegar and water. Add your favorite herbs and spices and cover tightly. Refrigerate for at least 3 days before using.

Vinegar-Pepper Sauce Supreme

Place an assortment of small whole red and green peppers (or sliced large ones) in a decorative bottle. Use sweet peppers for a mild sauce, hot peppers for a tangy one. Add a couple green onions and a small leek. Fill the jar with apple cider vinegar which has been heated to the boiling point. Cap the jar and set aside for at least a month.

Use vinegar-pepper sauce on salads (especially pasta salads), to add zing to vegetable dishes, and to enliven meats. Add a Mediterranean flavor to the pepper sauce by adding a few cloves of garlic to the basic pepper and onion recipe.

Herbs & Vinegar

Make herbal vinegar by adding 1/4 to 1/2 cup fresh (or 1 to 2 tablespoons dried) herbs to a small bottle of vinegar. Use apple cider or white vinegar, depending on the flavor wanted. Let the herbs soak in the vinegar for a month, shaking the jar every few days. Strain before using, or not. For a special look, strain out the bits of herb, then put a sprig of fresh herb in the finished vinegar. It will add to the flavor, and it looks great for vinegar which is used for gifts.

Herbal Vinegars

Herbal vinegars can be prepared easily by simply adding fresh or dried herbs to white, wine or apple cider vinegar. Let the herbs steep in the vinegar for 2 to 4 weeks before using. Herbs may be strained out, or left in.

Many different herbs can be used for making vinegars. Use a single herb, or combine several to create your own special blend. Choose herbs for their flavor and compatibility with other foods. Some herbs to try, and the special qualities they bring to herbal vinegars follow:

Anise

This relative of fennel has a sweet, licorice-like taste and pretty fernlike leaves.

Bay

Leaves of the sweet bay tree are shiny and dark green. Their flavor goes well with meats.

Use this to make bay-rum after shave.

Ginger

A small piece of ginger adds a lot of flavor. Use this unusual tasting condiment in Oriental dishes.

Horseradish

Slivers of horseradish root produce a vinegar with an especially zippy flavor.

Sweet Marjoram

This Old World herb is very strong and makes a vinegar that can pep up a bland stew or soup.

Other herbs for making vinegars are dill, basil, rosemary, mint, catnip, lemon balm, sage, tarragon, caraway and thyme. Combine several herbs to create your own special flavors. Then add a dash of cloves, allspice, nutmeg or cinnamon.

Herbal Vinegar Shortcut

A quick and easy way to prepare herbal vinegar is to add a herbal tea bag to a bottle of vinegar. Let it age, just as you would fresh or dried herbs, then remove the tea bag before using. (Or leave it in if you do not mind the way it looks.)

Garlic Flavored Vinegar

2   garlic cloves   2 cups vinegar

Place peeled cloves in apple cider vinegar and let set for at least a week. For a more robust vinegar, use additional garlic cloves.

Puckery Pickles

For truly tart and sour pickles, give them an extra helping of vinegar. Begin with a jar of whole dill pickles. Drain off the pickling juice and discard it. Next, cut the pickles into thin slices and put them back into the jar. Fill the jar with white vinegar and refrigerate for 5 days before eating. Pure puckery pleasure!

Tasty Pimientos

Pimientos are merely pickled sweet peppers! Make your own by thinly slicing sweet red peppers, blanching them to soften, and soaking in vinegar.

3/4 cup vinegar	dash of salt
3/4 cup water	4 garlic cloves
1/4 cup sugar	2 red peppers
1 teaspoon olive oil	

Simmer everything for the pimientos except the garlic and peppers for 10 minutes. Put the garlic and thinly sliced peppers into a glass jar, pour the hot liquid over them and marinate for 3 weeks. Enjoy! For an interesting change, use green peppers, or mix red and green half and half for a bright holiday look.

Chutney

Chutney is made by combining chopped vegetables, fruits and spices in a sweet pickling liquid. Originally, it came from India, where it was made with mangoes, raisins, tamarinds, ginger, spices. In the United States and England it is more likely to be made with tomatoes, apples, gooseberries, peaches, or bananas. Serve chutneys with cold meats.

Vinegar-Nut Pie Crust

1/2	cup butter	1/2	cup ground nuts
3/4	cup flour	2	tablespoons sugar
3/4	cup oatmeal	1	tablespoon white vinegar

Melt the butter in a pie pan and then add all the other ingredients. Mix with a fork, then pat the dough into shape. Bake for 15 - 20 minutes at 350°, fill with fresh fruit and a cornstarch based sauce.

Easiest Vinegar Pie Crust

1 1/3	cup flour	1	tablespoon vinegar
1/2	teaspoon salt	1/3	cup oil
2	tablespoons sugar	2	tablespoons water

Put all ingredients in a pie pan and stir with a fork until the flour is barely moist. Use the fingers to press and smooth the dough onto the sides and bottom of the pie pan, forming a fluted edge along the top. Prick with a fork and bake at 350° until lightly browned. (Or add filling and bake.)

White Vinegar Taffy

2	cups sugar	1	tablespoon butter
3	tablespoons white vinegar	1	teaspoon vanilla extract
1/2	cup water		

Combine sugar, vinegar and water and boil to the hard ball stage. Add butter and vanilla an stir just to mix. Pour onto a greased plate or counter top. When cool enough to touch (but still hot) begin to knead with buttered hands. When the taffy lightens and begins to firm up, cut ropes into small pieces. Wrap in waxed paper to keep it from becoming sticky.

Make honey taffy by replacing half of the sugar with honey. Make butterscotch taffy by replacing half of the sugar with brown sugar, increase the butter to 2 tablespoons.

Teresa's Peanut Butter-Vinegar Fudge

1	cup chocolate chips	1/4	cup corn syrup
3 1/2	cups sugar	1	tablespoon white vinegar
1 1/2	cups evaporated milk	3	cups peanut butter
1/2	cup butter	1	cup marshmallow cream

In a large saucepan, combine sugar, milk, butter, corn syrup and vinegar. Cook over medium heat, stirring constantly until mixture comes to a full boil. Boil and stir for 5 minutes, then remove from heat. Add the peanut butter and marshmallow cream and stir until smooth. Pour half of the hot mixture into a bowl with the chocolate chips and stir until smooth. Pour it into a wax paper lined pan. Top with the remaining hot mixture, allow to cool, then cut into squares.

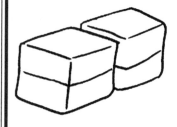

1½ cup milk is a 12 oz. can.

Chapter Nine

Odds & Ends

Vinegar —

Weed   An herb in the same family as peppermint.

Tree   A source of acid berries that can be used to make vinegar.

Eel   A harmless, threadlike worm that sometimes be found vinegar.

Bible   The result of a 1717 misprint in Oxford, England by Clarendon Press.

Vinegar is a weed, a tree, an eel and a Bible! Vinegar also has terrific versatility as a cleaner and neutralizer of caustic substances. On the pages which follow, you will see its usefulness on shoes, furniture, floors, luggage and much more!

Renew Suede Shoes
Put 2 cups water and 1/4 cup white vinegar in a pan and heat to the boiling point. Set heat to simmer and, while holding each shoe in the steam, gently brush up the nap. Set the shoes aside until completely dry before wearing.

Stay-Tied Trick For Leather Shoelaces
Leather shoestrings are notorious for their inability to hold a knot. The next time you want leather shoelaces to stay tied, put 3 drops of apple cider vinegar on the knot and give it an extra tug. The laces will stay tied until you untie them.

Setting Dye
After cloth has been treated with a commercial dye, soak it for an hour or two in a gallon of water, which has had a cup of white vinegar and a tablespoon of salt added to it. Rinse in cool water.

Red Dye

    1/2   cup vinegar
    1   pound beets
    1   quart water

Wash a pound of fresh beets and place them, with their skins on, in a sauce pan and cover with cool water. Simmer until the beets are tender, then remove skins. Chop the beets and return them to the same water in which they were cooked. Let them set for 2 hours, then strain off the liquid and add the vinegar. Use this liquid to turn cloth a warm, rose color.

End Squeaky Floors

    Quiet noisy wooden floors by forcing a mixture of vinegar and liquid soap into the cracks between boards. To each cup of liquid soap, add 2 tablespoons vinegar and mix well.

Old-Fashioned Wallpaper Paste

    1/2   cup cornstarch   6   cups boiling water
    3/4   cup cold water   1/4   cup white vinegar

Mix cornstarch and cold water and stir, all at once, into boiling water. When the mixture boils again remove from heat, pour through a strainer and stir in the vinegar. (This also makes a great laundry starch!)

Peel-No-More Painting

    Concrete walls and floors will take a coat of paint without troublesome peeling if the surface is first painted with vinegar. Brush on the vinegar, let the concrete dry, then paint as usual. This works on metal, too!

Paint Brush Renewal

    Old, stiff paint brushes can be restored to their former softness by removing dried-in paint. Simply put paint stiffened brushes in a small saucepan and cover them with full strength vinegar. Bring to a boil and simmer for 15 minutes. When cool enough to touch, work the softened paint out of the bristles under hot running water. Repeat as necessary. (Wood handled brushes are better candidates then plastic handled ones which may distort when heated.)

    Dry paint brushes by shaking them or spinning them between your palms. Do not stand brushes on their bristles, as that will ruin their shape.

Painted Windows

    Make removing paint from window glass easier with this trick. Mix a good, thick liquid detergent half and half with white vinegar. Spread this over the paint and allow to almost dry. Then remove the paint with a plastic scraper or a razor blade. The thick detergent helps keep the vinegar from running off, and together they soften the paint so that it comes off easier.

Tape Remover

A compress of vinegar will loosen the sticky glue on adhesive bandages, making removal less painful. Vinegar also softens the adhesives on masking, duct, strapping and other tapes.

Glue Removal

Most glues can be softened by soaking them in full strength vinegar. Add a drop of liquid detergent to help vinegar penetrate faster.

Better Humidifying

Add a couple of tablespoons of white vinegar to the water in a humidifier to eliminate odors in the home. Vinegar will also discourage the growth of germs in the humidifier's water reservoir.

Cleaning the Humidifier

At least once a week, soak the water reservoir for 10 minutes in a solution of 1 part white vinegar to 10 parts water. The vinegar will help to dissolve minerals salts, allowing them to be washed out so there is no buildup on the inside of the humidifier.

Instant Humidifying

Keep a 12 oz. pump spray bottle (the kind hair spray comes in) filled with water and 2 teaspoons white vinegar. These pump sprays deliver a very fine mist which is ideal for putting moisture into the air. Whenever a room is too dry, several pumps of the sprayer will provide an instant improvement in the humidity level.

Flavorful Humidifying

Any time vinegar is added to water to moisturize the air, you have the choice of using white, apple cider, or even an aromatic herbal vinegar. White is best if it is being used where there is some possibility of it settling on anything that could be stained.

If this is not a consideration, consider using a vinegar with a bit more 'spirit.' Apple cider vinegar adds a fresh, apple scent. Or, experiment with the many aromatic herbs that can add their unique fragrances to the moisture being put into the air.

Cleaning the Dehumidifier

Clean the water collecting tray with a brush dipped in full strength vinegar. If it is cleaned regularly, minerals will not build up in the tray and clog the outlet.

Better Dehumidifying

Put a splash of white vinegar in the dehumidifier's water collecting tray to discourage the growth of germs. This will keep the water from smelling stale and mildewy. (It will make cleaning easier, too!)

Air Cleaners

Air cleaners collect dust and other allergens. A cotton swab, dipped in water and vinegar, is good for cleaning hard to reach crevices and contact points. Fan blades need to be carefully wiped off, too.

Aquariums

A mild vinegar and water solution is the ideal substance for cleaning the outside of glass aquariums. Spray a soft cloth with a weak vinegar and water mixture (1 cup water, 1 teaspoon vinegar) and wipe surfaces until completely dry.

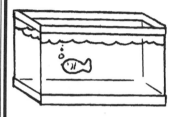

Very dirty aquarium glass can be scrubbed with a cloth wrung out of full strength vinegar. Rub dry with a soft cloth. Never spray aquarium glass, because fine droplets of mist can settle into the water and disrupt its the delicate ph balance.

Carpet Cleaner

    1   cup white vinegar
    1/4   cup rubbing alcohol
    1   teaspoon liquid detergent

Mix well, then pat gently onto soiled spots. Blot off and rinse with clear water. Repeat as necessary.

Wallpaper Stripper

To each cup of vinegar, add 1 tablespoon liquid detergent. Spray or wipe this solution onto walls and allow to set a few minutes. Most papers will scrape off easily.

Wood Scratches

Repair scratches in wood furniture with vinegar and a fresh walnut! Wipe the scratched area with a cloth dampened in full strength vinegar. Crack open a walnut and immediately rub the scratch with a piece of the kernel.

Water Resistant Furniture Polish

To encourage wood furniture to resist water spills and spatters, polish it with a mixture made of 1/2 cup lemon oil and 1 tablespoon white vinegar. Wipe the oil and vinegar on, then buff it off with a clean cloth.

Wet-Dry Vac

Half fill a pail with warm water and a cup of vinegar. Suck this solution up into the shop vac to clean and deodorize it. Let the warm liquid set for 3 minutes, then dump the water out and wipe the inside of the vac clean. Allow to air dry before putting it back together. Keeping the unit clean will extend the life of filters and prevent foul odors.

Plastic Wall Tile

Plastic tile scratches easily and attracts hard water mineral buildup. Clean it with non-abrasive white vinegar.

Plastic Food Containers

These storage containers pick up and hold food odors very easily. Keep them odor-free by soaking them in sudsy warm water, with a generous splash of white vinegar added to it.

Refrigerator and Freezer Gaskets

Wipe the gaskets around refrigerator and freezer doors with a mild detergent solution to keep them free of dirt and grease. If mold begins to form on the gaskets, remove it with white vinegar, then rinse with clear water before drying.

Window Shades and Blinds

Keep shades and blinds clean and free of smudges by wiping them down regularly with a cloth dampened in a mild vinegar and sudsy water solution.

Molded Plastic Luggage

Hard-sided suitcases can be cleaned with a solution made of half gentle liquid detergent and half white vinegar. Follow with a clear water rinse before buffing dry. Remember, handles need cleaning, too.

Play-Clay

1	cup flour	1	teaspoon vinegar
1/2	cup salt	1	tablespoon oil
1	cup water		

Combine all ingredients in a saucepan and heat. Stir continually, until it forms a ball. Remove from heat, allow to cool, then knead until smooth. A few drops of food coloring may be worked into it while kneading. Store between uses in a tightly sealed container in the refrigerator.

Flavorful Mouthwashes

A glass of water with a couple of teaspoons of vinegar in it is a traditional mouthwash and gargle liquid. Use white vinegar for a neutral taste, apple cider vinegar for its healing reputation, or herbal for breath enhancing flavor. Some good herbal vinegars for mouthwashes are sage, raspberry, peppermint and lavender.

No one book could ever contain all the useful remedies, cleaning shortcuts, and secrets of the good people I've met through my travels. Most likely you, too, know about healing remedies that have been passed down from generation to generation.

And so, I would love to hear from you. If you have a remedy, or other useful advice, you would like to share with others, please use this page (or a sheet of plain paper) to share it with me.* If I am able to use it in an upcoming edition of a remedies book, I will send you a free copy of the new book.

Thank you, and my best wishes for a long and healthy life,

Emily Thacker

_____

_____

_____

_____

_____

Please indicate (yes or no) whether I may use your name if I use this helpful advice:

❑ YES, please credit this remedy to _____
(Please Print)

❑ NO, please use my remedy, but do not use my name in the book.
(Either way, Yes or No, if I use your remedy, I'll send you a free copy of the new edition of home remedies!)

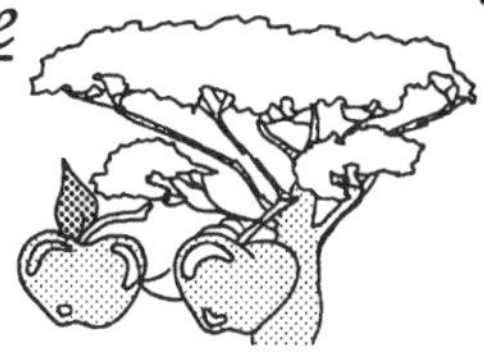

Your remedy can be one which uses vinegar or simply one that you feel others would like to know about.

Order Form

My favorite chapter in "The Vinegar Home Guide" is:

_____

_____

The helpful remedy I most appreciated in "The Vinegar Home Guide" appears on page
_____ , and tells how to: _____

_____

_____

What I liked best about "The Vinegar Home Guide" was:

_____

_____

_____

_____

If you have any comments or experiences to add to the information you've read in this collection, or if you have information for subsequent editions, please address your letters to:

Emily Thacker
718 - 12th Street N.W., Box 24500
Canton, Ohio 44701

- -

Use this coupon to order "The Vinegar Home Guide" for a friend or family member -- or copy the ordering information onto a plain piece of paper and mail to:

The Vinegar Home Guide
Dept. J8069
718 - 12th Street N.W.
Box 24500
Canton, Ohio 44701

Preferred Customer ReorderForm

Order this...	If you want a book on...	Cost...	Number of Copies...
Mind Power Memory Magic	New scientific breakthroughs promise Super Memory, yours at any age—Plus FREE bonus: Secrets of Pep, Vim and Vigor...	$9.95	
Home Remedies from the Old South	Hundreds of little known old-time remedies for aches & pains, cleaning & beauty.	$9.95	
The Garlic Book	Scientific discoveries backup old-time claims for garlic's ability to heal. Emily Thacker brings you a mix of old remedies, medical facts and healthy recipes.	$9.95	
FREE For Seniors	IT'S ALL FREE FOR SENIORS! Over 55? Every year Uncle Sam gives away millions of dollars in cash, goods and services to people just like you. Now, you can get your share regardless of your income.	$9.95	
CASH-It's On The House	How to get the most from your house. A new government benefit **guarantees** you the right to live in your home **AND** get tax-free cash for life!	$9.95	
The Vinegar Home Guide	The household edition to "The Vinegar Book" is now available! Learn how to clean and freshen with natural, environmentally-safe vinegar in the house, garden and laundry. Plus, delicious home-style recipes!	$9.95	
The Vinegar Book	Apple Cider Vinegar's magical mix of tart good taste and germ killing acid. Vinegar has more than 30 important nutrients, a dozen minerals, plus vitamins, amino acids, enzymes — even pectin for a healthy heart. And, there are hundreds of cooking hints.	$9.95	
The Vinegar Book II	What else can vinegar be used for? PLENTY! Brand new book gives you even more new and exciting ways to use vinegar for good health and natural healing. Discover how the combination of vinegar, honey & garlic can help relieve the pain of arthritis, reduce cholesterol, fight cancer, assist weight loss and MUCH MORE!	$9.95	

ny combination of the above $9.95 items qualifies for the ollowing discounts...

	Total NUMBER of $9.95 items	

Order any 2 items for: $15.95

Order any 3 items for: $19.95

Order any 6 items for: $34.95 and receive 7th item FREE

Any additional items for: $5 each

Order any 4 items for: $24.95

Order any 5 items for: $29.95

	Total COST of $9.95 items	

Order this...	If you want a book on...	Cost	Number of Copies
Emily's Vinegar Diet	This is the easy-to-follow diet you have been waiting for! It helps you lose weight without counting calories or being hungry. This time, you'll keep the weight off -- for life!	~~$10.95~~ $14.95	
Emily Thacker's Collected Works	Limited collector's edition of over 1,200 of Emily Thacker's best natural health folk remedies in a gigantic 8 1/2 x 11-inch volume. Four complete books cover home remedies for Vinegar, Garlic, Old South Home Remedies and alternative Health Without Drugs methods.	~~$29.95~~ $24.95	
	Postage & Handling		$2.95
	TOTAL		

90-Day Money-Back Guarantee

Please rush me the items marked above. I understand that I must be completely satisfied or I can return any item within 90 days with proof of purchase for a full and prompt refund of my purchase price.

I am enclosing $_____ by: ❑ Check ❑ Money Order (Make checks payable to Tresco)

Charge my: ❑ VISA ❑ MasterCard Card No. _____

Signature _____ Exp. Date _____

Name _____

Address _____

City _____ State _____ Zip _____

Telephone Number (_____)_____

For Faster Service
Credit Card customers call
TOLL FREE 1-800-772-7285
Operator Q1060

Mail To: TRESCO PUBLISHERS • 718 - 12th St. N.W., Box 24500, Dept. Q1060 • Canton, Ohio 44701
Customer Service (330) 453-8311

1998 TCO Q1312IM

MEMORY MAGIC

Is your memory as good as it once was? See how to remember more things longer, learn facts faster, make fewer mistakes and release the full power of your mind.

You need never lose your keys, forget where you parked your car or miss an important meeting. If forgetfulness has made your life miserable - you NEED Memory Magic.

FREE BONUS: SECRETS OF PEP, VIM AND VIGOR...

HOME REMEDIES FROM THE OLD SOUTH

Emily Thacker's original collection of old-time remedies. Hundreds of little-known cures from yesteryear on how to lose weight, beautify skin, help arthritis. A collection of more than 700 remedies Grandma used for colds, sinus, sexual dysfunction, gout, hangovers, asthma, urinary infections, headaches, and appetite control.

FREE BONUS: THE INCREDIBLE MAGIC OF HONEY & VINEGAR FOR HEALING, HEALTH & WEIGHT LOSS shows you how these two vitamin and mineral packed health foods have been used for better health, younger-looking skin, and safer cleaning.

THE GARLIC BOOK

Hundreds of little known old-time cures using garlic's almost magical ability to heal and protect. Medical science has lots to say about this wonderful little bulb, some of which may surprise you! Ways to use garlic inside and outside of the body, what's the best kind, and how to cultivate your own year round supply.

NEW

FREE FOR SENIORS

IT'S ALL FREE FOR SENIORS! Over 55? Or have a loved one who is? Here's how to get your share of free stuff from the government. One of America's best kept secrets is that you may qualify, (regardless of your income) for FREE prescriptions, medical & dental care, legal help, money for bill paying, free travel and hundreds of other government freebies.

CASH - IT'S ON THE HOUSE

If you are at least 62 years old and own your home you NEED TO KNOW about an exciting new program that supplies a monthly income, for the rest of your life, no matter how long you live! The Federal Government's Reverse Mortgage program allows home owners to tap into the value of their home and provides monthly income that need not be repaid as long as they live in the home. This cash will not affect Social Security payments, be taxed or counted as income. Are you cash poor and house rich? In an expensive-to-maintain, expensive-to-heat home, with a shrinking income? A Reverse Mortgage may be for you.

THE VINEGAR HOME GUIDE

Emily Thacker presents her second volume of hundreds of all-new vinegar tips. Use versatile vinegar to add a low-sodium zap of flavor to your cooking, as well as getting your house "white-glove" clean for just pennies. Plus, safe and easy tips on shining and polishing brass, copper & pewter and removing stubborn stains & static cling in your laundry!

THE VINEGAR BOOK

Emily Thacker's collection of old-time remedies has hundreds of ways to use vinegar for health & healing, cooking & preserving, cleaning & polishing. See how vinegar's unique mix of more than 30 nutrients, nearly a dozen minerals, plus amino acids, enzymes, and pectin for a healthy heart has been used for thousands of years.

NEW

THE VINEGAR BOOK II

You asked for it — Emily Thacker delivered! Still more ways to use vinegar – around the house – for your pets – in the medicine cabinet and some surprising vinegar facts! There's even good news on Vinegar's role in the fight against aging!

NEW

EMILY'S VINEGAR DIET

This easiest diet ever helps you lose pounds and inches, and keep them off! With a tonic of apple cider vinegar and honey there is no confusing calorie counting, food restrictions or expensive supplements. Increase your energy level while the pounds melt away. See how to use the "magic" of thermogensis to be thinner, look younger and feel more vigorous -- without depriving yourself of the foods you love!

EMILY THACKER'S COLLECTED WORKS — OVER 1,200 FOLK REMEDIES — NOW IN ONE GIGANTIC COLLECTOR'S EDITION

Imagine! You can own the Collector's Edition of the best-selling Vinegar Book, Home Remedies from the Old South, Emily's Book of Health Without Drugs and The Garlic Book-- all 272 pages in a huge 8 1/2 x 11-inch volume. Give your family and friends the gift of a longer, healthier, happier life for years to come.

All these important books carry our NO-RISK GUARANTEE. Enjoy them for three full months. If you are not 100% satisfied simply return the book(s) along with proof of purchase, for a prompt, "no questions asked" refund!